KEYS TO
EMPOWERING
OUR VOICES
THROUGH LIFE EXPERIENCES

KEYS TO
EMPOWERING
OUR VOICES
THROUGH LIFE EXPERIENCES

YVONNE DACRES

Published in 2023 by Yvonne Dacres

Copyright © Yvonne Dacres 2023
Yvonne Dacres has asserted her right to be identified as the author of this work in accordance with the Copyright, Designs, and Patents Act 1988

First published in the United Kingdom by Yvonne Dacres in 2023

A CIP catalogue record for this book will be available from the British Library

ISBN: 979-8-88759-551-1 (paperback)
ISBN: 979-8-88759-552-8 (ebook)

To Kimani and HP, who have been so patient and loving with me, plus the special people who believed in me even when sometimes I did not.

TABLE OF CONTENTS

SEEN BUT NOT HEARD
INTRODUCTION

Seen but not heard; I feel certain many of you can relate
Introduction to my life, but it was not my fate

I, Yvonne Elaine Dacres, came from an upbringing where children were seen but not heard. I will guess that you have heard many people say this if you were born in the mid-'60s, as I was. I say this lightly, but it was far from that. It was a very heavy, emotionless, and lonely place for me to be. It felt so lonely to the point where I did not feel like I was a part of my family. I felt more like an object than a human when expressing my views, opinions, and stances. What could I possibly have done with those feelings at such a young and tender age? Nothing, because I was dependent on those who cared for me. Unfortunately, they were busy getting acclimatised to this country. My feelings and what I had to say were not important. Thus, I found myself learning when and how to wear a mask and stifle what I felt. At such a young age, I never thought about how these beginnings would impact my life, but I learnt over time that the care my grandmother gave me was the best I could ever have asked for. She was the greatest person since sliced bread. I just did not recognise it at the time.

I know very little or nothing about my beginnings or how to emphasise my unimportance. No one ever talked about my baby stages, and I could not even find one baby photo of myself. The first and only photo I saw was of me standing between my mother and grandmother, where we looked dressed up to go out, and I was probably 3-5 years old. I took this lack of visibility (photos) personally, although I do not know how popular the camera was in those days. It may have been that the family did not own one. My heart ached because I did not live with my mother full-time. No one could understand how hurt I was. When I shared my concerns with my grandma, who we called Mama, she would always console me with some words which I knew were just to make me feel better.

Although I did not live with Grandma and Granddad from birth, I did move in with them before I started infant school at age 5. I stayed there until I transitioned to middle school. I was very upset that I had to live with Mama at the time, but it turned out that she was my saviour in disguise. Whatever love I felt was lacking from my biological mother, I received from Mama. I now see how Mama had a positive impact on my life.

As a baby, I sang with a hairbrush as a pretend microphone with my family as my audience. They told me I would always sing for anyone who would listen to me. Ironically, I did not feel heard, yet I would perform for my loved ones at the drop of a hat. My extended family members in London or elsewhere in England, plus my grandparents and close friends, had all heard me sing. I loved mingling with my cousins because I could be as silly as ever with them and not feel restricted or bored. I always sang at private birthday parties, christenings, and other special events until my cousin invited me to join a small group called The Faith Group. I thoroughly enjoyed this, even though performing in front of some big church audiences was nerve-racking. This was followed by a middle school performance where I became the narrator of the musical Joseph and the Amazing Technicolor Dreamcoat. One day I heard in a music class that the Music Department was getting ready to do auditions for their annual school show, and I was so prepared to sing. In those days, I was still young enough not to have any inhibitions. Subsequently, my attitude of "I am going to sing in this musical" is what landed me the role of the narrator, which I absolutely enjoyed. What added to this joy is that this was the first time I remember my mother coming out to watch me and appearing to be proud of me. Having been a performer for literally all my life, I naturally loved any music lesson I could be part of, whether in or out of school. At that young age, I was unaware that my whole life would be centred around music, even though everything I participated in required me to use my voice.

VARIOUS SINGING AND TRAINING EXPERIENCES

I thoroughly enjoyed my vocal experience as the narrator of the musical. At that time, I was sure that I wanted to pursue the field of music. Therefore, when I started high school, I approached the Head of Music about becoming a solo singer. She was insistent that I had to audition to be a choir member. I was unhappy because the school choirs and the music classes I had taken always sang classical music. Coming from a musical background of gospel, reggae, soul, and a little country music, I intuitively knew that this was not my path to becoming a famous solo artist. I shared my dilemma with my male Music/P.E. teacher, who laughed at me but realised I was serious. Upon this understanding, he offered to train my voice on the condition that I attended all scheduled lessons and was always punctual. He would create openings for me to sing whenever the school had a function for the teachers or parents.

At around age 17, I became a member of a girl band. I was extremely excited when a friend introduced me to a woman searching for a couple of singers to sing backup for her daughter. I believe this was fate. As a result, singing opportunities just kept opening for us. We named the band The Librians, as we were all the same Libra zodiac sign. We frequently met with Tracey King, the mother of one of the band members and a singer in her own right, for voice coaching to perfect our songs. It felt exhilarating to have space to express myself through voice because I no longer had to stay indoors and be bored with my surroundings. I now had a fresh musical family and space I could call my own. Even though it was awesome having our live band, a downside was that the members lacked punctuality. We were known to wait hours for the players to arrive, and there were rarely any apologies given. I was not overly concerned because I was doing what I loved: singing and adding value to the group. Creating harmonies was like the icing on the cake. I am not sure how the lead singer's mother got us the gigs, but we managed to do a lot of them.

The Jamaican Weekly Gleaner (EU) Wednesday, July 25, 1984

In my late teens, I decided that I wanted to sharpen my skills and keep my vocal ability strong by taking on a voice tutor. This was quite a different experience because I went from doing gigs at many different events to only singing when I went to my voice lessons. I stayed with Jilly, my voice tutor, for a couple of years, and upon reflection, I probably did this because I believed it to be the next best thing to fine-tune my vocal instrument. There was a lightness and loving feeling that I experienced when again, I was doing something that was for my benefit and enjoyment. I eventually decided that I wanted to do something different. That turned out to be, applying to audition for Sky Star Search, which was a TV talent competition. In this program, I had a

Streatham Guardian Series, Thursday, September 21, 1989

very big wake-up call to the fact that being in a room and singing with my voice coach would not give me the experience of singing to the world. I intended to sing at big events and become famous. Sky Star Search was one of my most embarrassing experiences ever, as the performance was televised to a large audience. I looked so well-groomed and made up, yet this was the worst I had ever performed the song because my nervousness destroyed my actual presentation. This was when I discovered that I needed to gain experience performing in front of audiences. After this act, I thought I could never show my face or perform in public again. I was so wrong because this forced me to attend a vocal school that would bring out the real badass champion in me.

I joined the Aria School of Voice after speaking to many vocal friends. I shared with them what I classified as my nightmare performance and that I needed somewhere new to voice train. I discussed with my tutor what I was going to do. Then I visited the school. From day one, I loved everything about it, even the drama. It was great. I was doing what I loved most: interacting vocally with a group of singers and improving my craft. I learnt how to stay focused, be disciplined, love our group like a family, show up fully committed, get paid, and be professional. We all learnt that you are as strong as your weakest link, so if one of us failed, we all failed. A failure would be deemed as not learning your song when you had to do a duet with someone or run up and down the stairs for eight sets when you knew ten sets were required. It was a very rigid process, as all newcomers would have to do the basics of singing for three months before we even sang a note. This would entail breathing, diction, posture, drama, and body conditioning. Looking back, I guess this sifted out the singers that were serious about their craft.

I remember being in rooms singing in harmony until 2:00 AM some mornings. We met for a minimum of two nights per week. The more coordinated we became in singing with each other, the more gigs per month our choir was invited to sing at. Even after years of training and being in the choir, I was still trying to sing solos from the back of the group where no one could see me. After our leader Eugene Thompson had seen my improvement, he released me from the vocal school. That was a gentle way of putting it. He dismissed me and said that I had done enough hiding and that it was time to go out and perform. Although I was out of the group, I kept up with private performances.

After the above, I took a different path in life, and with a five-month-old baby and a two-year-old son in tow, I went back to school in 1995 and did an Introduction to Music Course at Lewisham College. Having spent all my life doing things for approval or looking after others, this was the year that I decided that I was going to do something for myself, which was to study music. I had always had high respect for classroom teachers and knew up until this course that I would never be one. However, this was when I discovered I could be a teacher and decided to become one.

This had to be one of my toughest years of schooling due to the added responsibility of being a new, single mum to two young children. I had to rehouse because we lived in a one-bedroom flat. The system would not pay for my mortgage, or so they said, because I owned my property. I clearly could not get employment because I had two very young children. My son was only one month old, and I was still breastfeeding when we were in the process of moving. Understandably, I was not in the frame of mind to work. The estate agents could not seem to get me a sale, so I had no choice but to give back the keys. I was fortunate to have had help from the system to get my youngest boy into a nursery when I was at school and rehoused, which was the intention. But I was boarded in a very unsavoury area where they housed most single mothers. In October of that year, my youngest son's father agreed to babysit him for a couple of days per week while I was in college. One Sunday, not long after I had started my course, he called and left a message on my phone stating that he could no longer babysit. This meant as of the very next day, he could not take care of my son. As you can imagine, I was livid, and I was under stress about what I was going to do. Hoping that he would not be the mean person I now believed him to be, I took my son to his home anyway, but no one opened the front door. I was mad at him but continued to take my oldest son to his nursery, where they told me about a childminder that they had known other mothers to have used in the past. Therefore, I called in and notified my professor of why I would be absent that day. I organised a meeting with this Irish childminder that not only did I warm up to instantly, but she totally loved my son. Thankfully, the relationship between the three of us flowed as gracefully as I needed it to, if only for my sanity.

I lived about an hour from college. However, I had to start early in the mornings to do nursery and minder drop-offs before classes. I had little time to give any real attention to the anxiety and slight fear that I must have felt about returning to education as a mature student. I bypassed all of that and enjoyed myself so much that not only did I experience an impressive final performance and achieve great grades, but I also managed to achieve the Best Student of the Year award. This was not bad for a woman that had been out of the academic system for over ten years.

I watched and admired the professors and tutors who enjoyed teaching us and saw the pride in them when we did so well. I held umpteen conversations with them and then decided that although I did not want to teach in a school, I could still teach privately. Subsequently, in 1996 I followed up with an Introduction to Vocal Workshops Course, a class taken at Goldsmiths College, knowing that I would teach from home. I believe this was where I started to observe people and learn from what I saw. Whether these were things I wanted to do or not, it was a strategy that gave me my best learning. I continued over the summer, taking whatever weekend vocal courses I could find so that I would be able to transfer nothing but the best to my students. Two of those were Kodály courses, one specifically for teaching children, and another was about teaching vocals to babies in the womb.

I felt confident to show a bunch of people how to sing, but I wanted to do more than show them. I wanted what they learnt from me to have an impact on their own lives as well as their performances. Consequently, I decided to find a college that would be able to teach me that skill. As a result, in 1998, I started a Certificate in Education at Croydon College, which would lead me to this goal. This class met for three hours one morning per week at my local college. Upon reflection, I could see that doing as many courses as I did that year was pretty sadistic. On top of the Certificate in Education, I started a Kodály Course that fortunately met during the evenings. Then on top of that, I found out that the Government support system was offering a course specifically for musicians, so you can imagine how I jumped on this opportunity. This was a music facilitator course that I did in Sanderstead. Again, this was part-time, but towards the end of the year, it got crazy. Croydon College taught me how to develop and customise a curriculum for my future students. The course was 100% classroom based. The Kodály school was developing my musicianship and showing me that I was more capable of sight-singing and playing the piano than I thought. My favourite course was the facilitator course. Because not only was I learning with musicians of different instrumental backgrounds, but I was also gaining a diverse type of experience. Plus, I could sing and work at Croydon High Private School, where we had heaps of fun. I created an opportunity to prepare the girls from the High school for their final performance of the year. I managed to get a band together from the musicians on my course, and we rocked it. Even though there was a Football cup final on the night of our performance, the dads were still there. I guess this showed how excited and confident the girls were about the show they were due to present. It made such an impact that the local newspaper also came down to take a photo and do a write-up about the positive things they had heard about "Soul's in Their Eyes." It was not all sweetness and light because the older students came to some of my coaching sessions and mocked me.

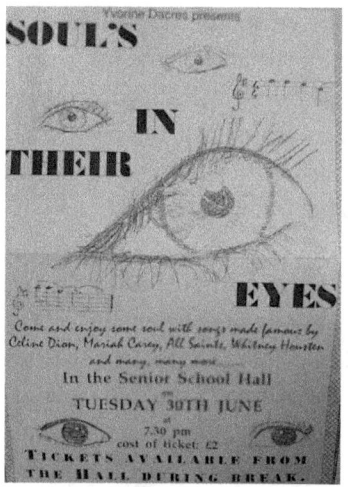

AS DESIGNED BY THE STUDENTS

The Advertiser July 10, 1998

I was learning that it did not even make sense to get mad at people who do you wrong because what goes around comes around. It turned out that their concert was a flop, and the performances were not particularly great either. Then the next time the older students went to lessons, the music teachers made it very clear to them how successful our performance was. I guess this was the consequence of their actions. At the end of this course, I had to produce a 30-week course of my own to present to my future students. This came in very handy as I would go on to start my own business before I had completed my Certificate of Education Course.

God always sends something or someone to place me on track. Just as She made me aware of the Facilitator Course, God then made me aware of an Entrepreneur Course that was again held by the system and would guide me into self-employment. It was a three-month course, and what I remember most is being told every week the number of benefits we would lose. To be honest, this man did not phase me because I knew in my heart there was no way I would fail, and that this new business would do well. By 1999, I had officially opened my Yvonne Miller School of Voice business. Having comfortably come off the system's support, I knew where I wanted to go with my business. An advertisement in the local sweet shop window was the only ad I had ever placed for private students, and I achieved a couple of clients from that ad. After that, I just spoke to people about my business, and other clients came to me by word of mouth. There was always someone who had ideas, and I just followed up on those suggestions. I ended up working with schools of all ages, colleges, performing arts departments, churches, and art schools. The private clients at home came in handy when I needed assessments for my Certificate of Education; fortunately, I did well on them. By my final year, I found a part-time lecturing job at my college, which enabled me to complete my assessments as most of the work I was doing before this had dried up. So, you can say I just kept doing what I did well: communicating with people. I would speak to Heads of Schools, Heads of Music departments, Choir Directors, and whoever I felt needed my expertise because I was ready by then.

There was also the performing side of my business, where I performed whenever I saw an opportunity. I found that few people paid me, which I related to not having found the power behind my voice. I had a beautiful voice. I understood this because whenever people complimented me on my performance, this is what they always stated. Although I had worked my way through all the previous challenges in my life to be able to share myself as a voice coach and a voice artist, I still believed my voice to be unworthy of payment. I felt I had not worked on myself enough to truly see the beauty in myself or my voice that others saw back then. There was still that part of me that had learnt to make people happy, but not myself. Because I felt that way, any kind-hearted things people said to me were never taken seriously. I felt they said it because they wanted to say something to the singer, not because they had heard a beautiful voice.

I always had a dream that I wanted to live in the USA, if only for a period of my life. From that dream, I started working on that GOAL at least five years before leaving the country. This worked for me at the time because I wrote down a list of what I wanted to achieve over the year. Then on a new page for each goal on that list, I would write out steps I thought I needed to take to achieve them. Then, as of the next day, I would start working on those lists. Goals were written and attacked with gusto at the beginning of the year, followed by not even looking at them for at least a month. This was usually the case, but what I found in most cases was that even though I did not follow the steps religiously, at least ninety per cent of those goals were achieved. I now realise there is truth to writing down what you want to accomplish because they materialise just how God wants them to, not you.

2

GOALS: MINE, AND WRITING YOURS

Goals of Mine and help with writing Yours
Without them, I always found life resulted in a long pause

I registered for a course on how to set goals and how to focus on achieving them. I noticed that my goals were accomplished when I focused on all the steps. The real key was to remain attentive to each goal because once you dropped the energy, the goal dissipated, although this did not happen all the time. We were taught the following five steps. The goals were achieved more when I deliberately approached them with conviction. In some cases, my fear reduced the energy I needed to achieve a specific goal. As a result, I did not complete that goal.

THE END OF THE MOVIE

Pretend that how you see your goal resembles that of an award-winning ceremony. Then write a paragraph about how this plays out. If you can visualise your end goal, you are already on the way to succeeding. Writing it in paragraph form gets your creative juices flowing about how much it means to you and raises your belief in that goal. Finally, state what your goal looks like when it is accomplished so that you can create and see what it looks like with the following in mind:

For this exercise, my primary goal was my dream to live in America.

Example: I am dressed in my cap and gown. I am feeling extremely nervous. The immediate and most important members of my family and friends surround me. I walk across the stage to receive my certificate, and much of the crowd applauds my success. This is due to the number of friends and associates I gained over the years while at Spelman. I feel extremely proud of myself, and my walk could not be more peppered with confidence. After graduation, there are many smiles and happiness, not just because it is over but because my friends, family, and associates are also very proud of me. I go home to a smaller gathering of people who celebrate my achievement with love, comfort, and pride.

WHEN?

Give yourself a completion date and write it down (preferably in a journal or a calendar).

For example, do you have to perform or speak on a certain date? If so, come up with a date by which you want to know the song, to the best of your ability, at least a month in advance.

Example: I knew I had to be in the USA to start school by <u>Wednesday, the 18th of August</u>, so I worked with this date to the best of my ability. I also gave myself a deadline of the 15th of June. If I did not have the money by then, I would not pursue this goal this year.

WHERE?

Think of a place where you dream or desire to perform or speak at, then make this your where?

Example: I had always known (daydreamed) the United States as where I wished to live abroad, which made this my where? Atlanta, Georgia, turned out to be the specific city and state, but I was happy about this as I was not so concerned about the area of the States. However, I will stress that this part of the process works well when you are as specific as possible.

WHAT?

Think about the thoughts that brought this goal to mind and led you to the decision to make this objective a goal. Then write down exactly what it is that you want.

Example: I wanted to live in the US, and through making many inquiries, including the visa lottery, I decided that a very legitimate way to gain entry was as a student, so this is the avenue I chose. Each year I wrote down that I would do whatever was necessary to achieve this goal. Whether it was inquiries about workshops, funding, scholarships, or visas, these were the things I kept doing until I knew how to fund what I wanted. So, my answer to what, was that I wanted to do a music course of some kind.

WHY?

Why did you choose to perform at this event to fulfil this goal? What do you think you are going to get from attaining it?

Example: For me, going to live in the states at some stage of my life had always been a dream. I believed that the Bachelor of Arts Degree in Music Performance would benefit my career and thus help my future students, as I would gain more experience to share with them. Also, as far as my business was concerned, my students were always a priority.

HOW?

Preparing to Leave to Live abroad

Writing down the steps to be taken would give you your how. You could do this in either of the following two ways. Firstly, start with what you can do right now, immediately after you finish typing or writing. Then write every-thing you want and need to put into place until you accomplish your goal. The other option is, to begin with, the last thing you would do on your list when you finished typing.

Here are some examples of what was on my list when I felt it was time to proceed:

- Connect with the appropriate college department to find out about the application process to become a student there.
- Seek a tutor to prepare for the SATS exams and submit results to the school.
- Find places that may give scholarships or help me with funding.
- Provide the school with the paperwork needed for my application and visa.
- Get websites for real estate agents that could show me properties for us to live in.
- Get in contact with the family who offered to house us until we had what we needed in place to settle in Atlanta. Us being my nine and eleven-year-old sons and, of course, me.
- Find out what vaccinations I needed to start school so I could have them done here in the UK for free.
- Get the full physical required from my doctors as proof that I was in good enough health to be a student abroad.
- Also, get the x-rays required as part of the physical that doctors at the hospital had approved.
- Get an application and apply for a financial loan.
- Get my credit cards in a healthy condition to take care of big items like furniture and a car when I arrive in the US.
- Have a conversation with my uncle to make sure he is still comfortable with staying in and maintaining our home while I was abroad. Plus, work out how he could pay me for my car in instalments.
- Use the I20-document sent from the college to book my appointment for a visa interview at the American Embassy.
- Download, fill out, and pay for the visas to make the appointment.
- Get up-to-date pictures for our visas.
- Transfer bills into my uncle's name while we were away from my home.
- Cancel any financial support I received from the system.
- Book flights.

- Start packing as soon as possible.
- Make inquiries for school requirements for my boys.
- Look for good schools and ask to view properties in that area.
- Register for an online mortgage or rental company account to ensure monthly payments are maintained.
- Make sure the loft is cleared out as much as possible. This was the last issue I wanted to deal with as the departure date drew near.
- Pack boxes with the things I wanted to ship to the states.
- Then research shipping companies and get boxes posted to the US.
- Get a plastic folder for all the important documents I would accumulate and need to keep safe, such as:
  - Passports
  - I20's
  - Visas
  - I95

The above process is what I used to accomplish my goal of living abroad. And I can assure you this was achieved in the eight weeks I had from receiving a small loan to support my venture, to landing in the USA on Friday the 13th of August.

3

AREAS TO WORK ON YOUR VOICE

Areas to work on your voice, follow these keys to be empowered
I have broken this course down as much as possible,
so the journey won't be soured

ICE BREAKER

When working with a new student, I usually begin with a set of questions. These show me who you are and where you are coming from as far as your performances and presentations go. When working with a group, I will give the questions to pairs or even bigger groups, and then one group member will introduce the other/s with their findings. I would use fewer questions for groups, as the conversations that build could go on for hours if they had to answer all these.

If you are doing this exercise yourself, I recommend doing it with pen and paper in a quiet space so you can search, reflect, and understand who you are or what you have become. Specifically, it will help you focus on your intentions and where you want to take your goals.

1. ***When was the last time you performed/presented?***
    i.   Think about who invited/requested/commissioned you to perform.

    ii. Did you willingly/hesitantly/assertively accept? Do you look forward to singing/speaking for this person or client again?

    iii. If it has been long, why has it been so long since your last performance?

2. ***Think about this performance***
   i. Is this a location or a venue that you would present/perform at again?
   ii. Was it a solo or a group performance?
   iii. How did that go? Were you happy with the recital?

3. ***It is always best to video record your performances to be able to answer:***
   i. How did your last performance look?
   ii. Was there room for improvement?
   iii. What do you want to change to make it better?

4. ***What are your goals for the next six months? Examples could be:***
   i. I want to stand up and speak to the next audience I encounter, whether I am invited to do so or not.
   ii. If you are a smoker or a drinker:

       I want to monitor the amount that I am drinking or smoking now.

       If you drink five cans of beer a day, you may want to try four cans. If you can discipline yourself to bring it down by one can every four weeks, set the intention to do so. Same with cigarettes, if you smoke two packs daily, bring it down by at least two cigarettes a day. Here, you will be able to grow as you prove to yourself that you can do anything you want. Just set the intention.

   iii. I suggest that you reward yourself according to the amount of money you save, or better still, set up a direct debit to transfer that money you are keeping into a savings account.

BODY CARE

    i. How much harder your body works when it is not at ease is highly underestimated. Therefore, it is necessary to ensure that if your body is diseased, you find a way to resolve it, as this can surely impact your performance.

    ii. Do you suffer from physical problems?

Do a thorough check for yourself. Start listening to your body when you flinch, slow down, are fatigued, or feel constant aches and pain. These are signs that your body needs attention. One of the most underestimated cures is sleep. If you are getting four hours a night, gradually increase that number.

iii. Go and get checked by a doctor who is more into natural healing.

You can also use a conventional doctor, but just for a diagnosis, and see how you can help yourself instead of taking drugs produced by man.

iv. Find out your body's issues and get to work on them.

This could be done by using a:
a) Chiropractor
b) Herbalist
c) Counsellor
d) Naturopathic Doctors

These would be the type of people I would recommend. Using naturally grown things to fix and heal our bodies' ailments is always better than manufactured drugs.

LOOK AT/STUDY WHO YOUR FAVOURITE SPEAKERS/SINGERS ARE

i. Make a list of and start listening to your favourite singers—the more eclectic, the better. Put a playlist together so you can listen to those speakers while travelling. Then begin to note what it is you like about them.

ii. This is basically how you find your specific niche, and the more mixture there is, the more unique you become as an artist or speaker.

HOW COMMITTED ARE YOU TO THE PROCESS OF MAKING IT BIG?

i. For some people, it helps to think about how they would deal with success.

ii. Are you in fear of success or failure? Or does either way not bother you?

iii. If you could start earning vast amounts of money, do you already have plans for that money?

You may not be in this to be big, but if you are, the above three points would be something worth thinking about and planning for.

I like to familiarise myself with the client on how they want to better their current performance and/or protect their voices and share with them how they could help themselves improve their physicality. I then create a plan and make suggestions on how they could prepare for a career in singing or speaking. My next step is usually to start with breathing exercises as follows:

BREATHING

If you have not already done this, then reverse your breathing pattern. So, by this, I mean instead of sucking your stomach in when you breathe in, inflate it. Plus, when you breathe out, the stomach should now deflate. In this way, you have more air to support whatever sounds you want to create, and you will be able to lengthen and heighten notes with ease, thus eventually enhancing your performance.

The following pictures show how the diaphragm moves when breathing deeply:

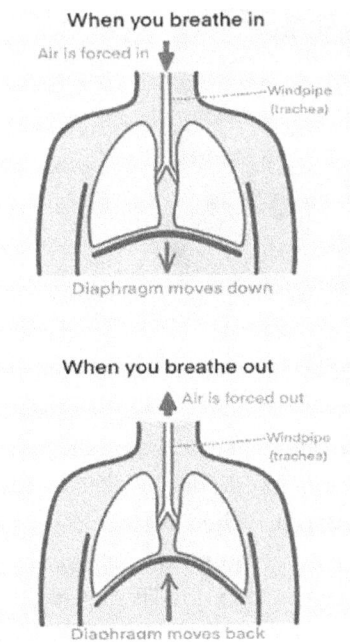

As the diaphragm pushes up, as shown above, it pushes out the air from your lungs. Then, as you inhale, the diaphragm muscle pushes down, making space for the lungs to fill up.

Breathing Exercises to help develop this way of breathing:

First, you want to get used to breathing in the above way by starting to practise little but often. I start my students on **two** minutes per day so they may practise every day instead of feeling guilty about not practising at all. As you add more exercises and develop a daily schedule, you will naturally work for more than **two** minutes. The eventual aim is to breathe in this way all the time so that when you sing or speak at your events, you are concentrating on performing your song, not how to breathe. You will stay focused on what your audience wants to hear, which is your song or speech.

<u>**Breathe in**</u> for 4 secs <u>**Hold your breath**</u> for 4 secs <u>**Breathe out**</u> for 4 secs

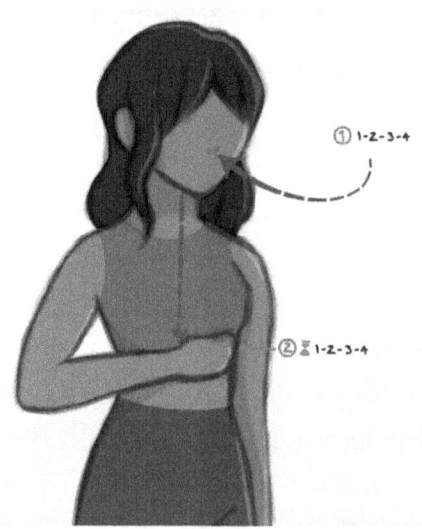

Increase the seconds—make sure your lungs are inflating and deflating while you count; otherwise, it will not be as effective in improving your breathing. For example, the tummy needs to be moving out for the full amount of time that you count to four. You do not breathe in and then count to four. Do the same when breathing out. When performing or speaking, you need the breath available as and when required to get the flow you want. You do not want to be gasping for breath when none is required.

An example I like to use to emphasise this is asking the students to say hello and introduce themselves. Then do this again but take a large breath before speaking. This would be unnatural, so why do it at the beginning of a song or a line, where it is clearly not required? This is not usually done intentionally; it is usually done because the singer/speaker has run out of breath. So, this is what we want to avoid.

Breathe out on:

- Single Breaths—these could be snatch, short or long breaths.
- Ahh
- Ooo
- Mmm
- Scales—if you sing them comfortably in tune.
- Lines from speeches you have heard and liked or one you propose to carry out.

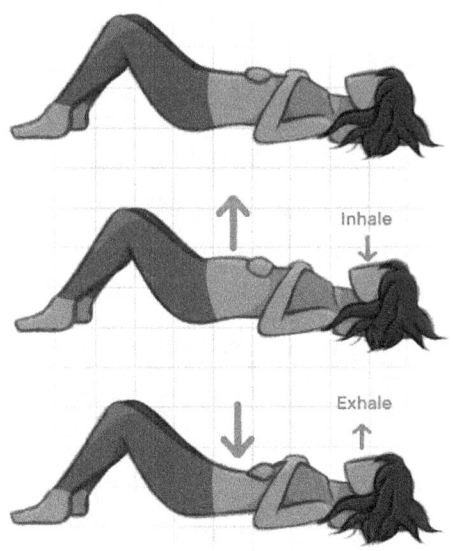

You can lay with your legs straight if you so wish, plus I use a CD or a book on their stomachs (as low down as possible) to help my students focus on pushing something up while breathing in. This is a good way to practise as it works more easily due to gravity. Then take this from horizontal to upright, as this is how you will sing.

As you get better and more confident at the above, add to the strength of it all by doing breathing exercises while lying on your tummy.

As you gain more control, do breathing exercises, sing your song, or do your speech with a candle in front of your mouth. Preferably, put the candle in a place that requires you to stand up, maybe on the edge of a mantelpiece or a mirror ledge in the bathroom. The flame needs to be in line with the air coming out of your mouth, but not too close. When you breathe, sing, or speak, the idea is for you not to blow out the candle during this process.

I teach breathing first because I believe it is the foundation of voice production and is very important. The reason for this rank is that without the support of the breath, you may not be able to create the sound you need.

SCALES AND ARPEGGIOS

These exercises can improve your sound and confidence immensely if practiced correctly. Not only can you use these to warm up vocally before a performance, but they keep the vocal muscles working so that they do not fail you when you do your presentation. You will be in a better position to project your voice with poise, precision, and skill.

Vocal exercises using the scale and or arpeggio:

Do Re Mi Fa Sol La Ti Do

Do Me Sol Do Sol Mi Do

Just as you would have to take responsibility for your next move in life, where I will not be face-to-face with you, I now expect you to research some short vocal exercises online and create a small program for yourself. For those who are competent with singing scales in tune, this will keep the muscles strong and healthy in preparation for when you are called upon to perform or present. However, for those who are not so confident—meaning you are constantly having people ask you to stop when you start singing. I suggest you start by singing two notes of the above scale at a time. Repetition is key. You may want to work with someone with a good ear that will be honest but not brutal about what they hear from you.

So, start on the first two notes of the scale—doh re, and when you are happy that you are singing what you hear, then sing the first three notes of the scale—doh re me. And repeat the process and keep adding the notes until you can sing a strong scale. Sing up the scale, down the scale, arpeggios, triads, and whatever other exercises you can find online.

I always recommend that you learn from a voice instead of a keyboard. Although, if you are forced to use the piano, use it for a limited amount of time, for example, for the first note of each scale or arpeggio. If you feel you are off-key, check your note with a keyboard or piano.

You can download a piano app on your phone. You do not have to purchase a piano or a keyboard, although it would be a great idea to have one to help with your song writing. The other great thing about the daily practice of scales, arpeggios, and other exercises you find is that they help you widen your octave range. I have shown you the middle C scales and arpeggios, but I advise you, as I do all my students, to start on your lowest note possible. This is after you have found strength and confidence in producing scales correctly. For example, each time you sing a scale—from your lowest note—the next time you sing a scale, you start it on the "re" of your previous scale. In doing this daily, you will find that the top notes that were once out of your reach will become much easier. Then, before you know it, what used to be a one-and-a-half-octave range, will soon become a three-octave range. Do this with all the vocal exercises you do, and this will give you little or no limit on the types of songs you can produce with comfort, poise, and grace.

DICTION

Have you ever been to an event where the artists had lost your attention because you did not know what they were singing about? There could be many reasons for this. Articulation of the lyrics is one reason. Therefore, I focus on diction with the artists I teach so that people can understand what they are singing and or speaking about.

Here are some short exercises that you can use to focus on your diction. To break this down, the different letters that we articulate are placed in different areas of the mouth, and the following are just a few examples.

CONSONANTS

Areas of the mouth	Also known as	Letters
Lips	Labials	M B P F V
Tongue	Linguals	L N R
Throat	Gutturals	C G
Teeth	Dentals	T D
Palatines	Soft Palate	Q K KWAK KEY
Whistling	Sibilants	S Z ZII ZED

1. When producing labials, the two letters to be wary of are the M and the F. When we speak or produce these sounds, we tend to put an /e/ sound on the front, as in the word ten. For this exercise, I will refer to it as a clicking sound. What we want to do instead of clicking is to use your breath to push out and give a smooth sound to these letters. Additionally, when pronouncing F and V, emphasise them as two different letters. Students tend not to separate them and end up sounding like the word hea-vy, so please be aware of this.

2. The clicking sound also occurs on the Linguals L and N, so remember to omit this by using your breath. Plus, you need to roll your R when you pronounce this letter—rrrr.

24

3. As the gutturals C and G are coming from the diaphragm, you want to push them out using exhalation as this gives more power. You will need to use one breath for each letter and do this quickly to help with breathing where you may need to take a snatched breath for a song.
4. For the dentals, make sure the tip of the tongue is touching your teeth. And the best way to do this is by closing your teeth together to produce clarity.
5. For the four sounds produced using the soft palate, you should find that the middle of your tongue touches the top of your mouth.
6. The whistling sounds are produced by emphasizing an S sound, whether on the S or Z letters or sounds. You should do these exercises slowly at first, ensuring you achieve the connections I tell you to make before putting and rolling them all together. The intention is to eventually sing/speak all the consonants and vowels in one breath, which helps when articulating words.

VOWELS

A   E   I   O   U

ITALIAN VOWELS

AH   EH   EE   OH   OO

With the vowels, you will find yourself pronouncing all of them with the clicking sound on the front. Just remember to use your breath to eradicate your click. You will know that you have it once you hear that smooth sound.

The idea of these exercises is to work in each section until you are comfortable with your articulation of all areas. Then roll them out as one line, and to help with breathing, eventually sing all the letters in one breath.

POSTURE

a. **Head**   This should not be held too far back or forward, or it can block your sound.

b. **Shoulders**   These should be in a relaxed position and dropped down. Breathing when the shoulders rise, usually indicates that you are breathing from the chest instead of the lower abdominal area.

c. **Arms**   These should also be relaxed to the point that if someone lifts your arm, it should drop down by your side like a deadweight.

d. **Hands**   If you are a nervous person, it is best not to hold paper or a microphone, as it creates tension in the body.

e. **Back/Torso**   To hold as upright or straight as possible. To allow the air to flow comfortably through the body and again to prevent tension.

f. **Knees**   These should be unlocked and in a soft position as opposed to being bent, also to avoid tension.

g. **Feet**   Parallel and shoulder-width apart to create a nice even balance.

You want your body to be relaxed and void of all possible tension to prevent you from singing from the throat. If you speak or sing from the throat for a long period, you can cause many vocal problems that could ultimately be to the detriment of your voice.

Additionally, when you sing and feel fatigued in the vocal area, it is normally due to tiredness. When you are tired, many of the above areas go into the comfort zone, which usually relaxes into a position that goes against the posture required to produce your best sound. So now that you know how to hold your posture to benefit your presentation, you can adjust your positioning to ease your discomfort or fatigue. The bottom line is ensuring you get enough rest and sleep, which helps with posture.

APPROACH TO THE SONG/SPEECH

Approach to the song or how to present your speech
It's not just to listen and repeat; at least, that is not all I teach

BREAKING DOWN A SONG

1. *Lyrics*—First, go online and copy and paste the lyrics to your song into a word file. Then listen to the song while looking at the lyrics and ensure that you have the lyrics that the artist is singing. Cutting and pasting is not enough because the lyrics could be written down by anyone, which means they are not always correct. You will find umpteen variations of some lyrics, especially in live versions, as the artist sometimes sings what they feel at the time of presentation. Then add that everyone is fallible, so sometimes lyrics are forgotten, and a professional artist always keeps singing, so they may add or change a word.

2. *Breathing*—Listen to where the artist takes each breath and make a note, as this is exactly where you will be taking yours. Decide on what symbols you will choose to make a note of these breaths. For example, wherever the artist takes a breath, what symbol will you put before or after that word? So, you may put a small letter 'B' for an average breath,

'SB' for a snatched breath, and 'LB' for a long breath. You will be the one to present the song, so the symbols you use are entirely up to you.

If you do not want to breathe where the artist takes a breath, this will be fine when you have nailed the song but for now, trust the process. The idea is that you learn it parrot fashion first and then make the song your own. When you think of not limiting yourself, you realise that you gain from looking at songs that you may not particularly like, as there is something to be learnt from every artist or speaker. You want to know the song or what you will say inside out. So that if for some reason you forget the words, the musicians mess up, you are distracted, or even left without the instrumentation you planned to sing with. You will have no worries because you know your song completely. I had a rather nerve-racking experience once when I turned up to sing at a venue and was told that the sound engineer had failed to turn up, so there was no way to play my backing track. Sitting in the audience was the original singer of the song I was due to perform at that event. Fortunately, I knew my song without the music, so I was able to sing it anyway, but this is what I mean by being prepared.

3. *Diction*—We also want to note how the artist articulates their words so that we can copy this too. For instance, if they say **lovin'**, this is what you write/type because if you put **loving**, this could change the song's vibe, phrase, or meaning.

   Again, we copy the artist initially because while developing our own style/s, we want to practise how others present or perform their pieces. This will give us the confidence to sing all types of repertoires, thus removing limits on what we can perform or present.

4. *Phrasing*—We will make notes of the areas where lines or words are not sung straight but phrased in a specific way. Eventually, you will phrase the song or speech in your way. Again, choose how you want to note the phrases. It could be done by highlighting, underlining, leaving a space in a word, drawing an arrow to take a note up, or an arrow down. I may use a broken line to emphasise that a note is sung using vibrato or a solid line to show that a note is long and straight. This, again, is a personal choice because when you start to sing the song/speak the piece, you will have to remember the key you created.

5. *Instruments*—We will make a note of the actual instruments that are in the song you are studying. This will be done in a quiet environment where you can listen attentively to the instruments you are familiar with. If not, go online and listen to the sounds that instruments produce if you are not used to certain ones. Piano, guitar, and drums may be straightforward, but there are many stringed, brass, woodwind, keyboard, and percussion instruments within each family. Then repeat this exercise in a silent (if possible) environment with lights off, eyes closed, and see if you missed anything. The reason for doing this part of the exercise with the lights off is that when you remove your sense of sight, your hearing is heightened. And the interesting thing is that you nearly always hear instruments you did not hear before while listening with the light on. This is important because not only will you begin to learn the instruments that you are working with, but you will understand how they are structured around the lyrics of the song you are studying.

6. *Colours*—We will look at a song that can be coloured and make a note of how those colours impact the piece. A good example is that if someone was singing a sad song at a funeral, you might colour it dark blue with a solemn facial expression to match. But if that person sang it happily with a sunny yellow feeling and a smiling expression, this colour would not match what they were trying to portray. This could help you stay on track with the story you are trying to tell through your song or speech.

7. *Grammar/Storyline*—You must write out what the song means to you personally. Because what you need to understand is that if there are one thousand people in your audience, they will all have their own interpretation of your song or presentation. Subsequently, you will have to know from your interpretation of the song or speech what you want to say to the audience. Additionally, consider how the audience may feel about what you are saying. Also, when you are ready to perform/deliver, it will be presented with true meaning.

This can also be done in a way to help you remember the lyrics to your song. I suggest to my clients to write the song out, and alongside every line, write what it means to them.

Example: Run to You by Whitney Houston (a verse and chorus)

I wanna run to you (ooh)	I want to run to that special someone
I wanna run to you (ooh	I want to run to him
Won't you hold me in your arms	Please hold me in your arms
And keep me safe from harm?	Keep me safe from harm
I want to run to you (ooh)	Emphasis on running to him
But if I come to you (ooh)	She wants to know what will happen if she does
Tell me, will you stay or will you run away?	Will he stay, or will he leave her
Each day, each day I play the role	She acts out her life, making it out to be happy
Of someone always in control	Acting like she is always in Control
But at night I come home and turn the key	When she gets home and turns the key
There's nobody there, no one cares for me.	There is no one there to care for her
Oh oh, what's the sense of trying hard to find your dreams	She sees no point in chasing her dreams
Without someone to share it with?	When there is no one to share those dreams with
Tell me what does it mean?	She wants to be told what this all means

DEVELOPING LISTENING AND HEARING SKILLS

Breaking down the song forces you to listen intently, so in addition to that, you may want to do the following. This is not just to lock your song lyrics into your memory securely, but also to listen with the awareness and new knowledge that your performance could change yours or someone else's life. If you reflect on some of the things you have missed out on in life, for example, someone made you an offer you did not accept, and later the opportunity was no longer available. You then became very upset because you discovered that you were given a chance where you did not listen keenly to the offer. Also, you missed someone's cry for help, and having missed it, you ended up losing a friendship.

First, consider what makes up a song, such as lyrics, melody, rhythm, harmonies, instruments, verses, chorus, middle eight, and structure. And, of course, the areas addressed in breaking down the song.

Just as a speaker would want to look at the flow within her speech, she wants a high-impact beginning and end, plus to keep her audience engaged during the flow of the middle. A singer also wants to look at the structure of their song just- as attentively.

Examples:

Before doing this, work out how many beats you hear to each bar of your song, and this will help you work out the following:

Intro	= how many bars? What instrument/s introduces the song?
Verse	= lasts for how many bars?
Chorus	= lasts for how many bars?
Verse	Are these all phrased the same throughout? If not, what colours are used to change the sound of the melody?
Chorus	Listen for the tones in the singer's voice, as they will help you when working on your unique sound. This applies to colours as well.
Middle 8	= lasts for how many bars? Is this sung, or is it instrumental?
Chorus	Is the full chorus sung at the end?
Outro	Does the singer sing throughout the end of the song?

This last exercise gives you an edge in your performance. Look up and play at least two versions of the song you are working on to see how differently each artist presents a song. You can pick up ideas, twist them, enhance them, and play with them.

The speaker would look at the time they were given to speak and arrange what they would say over that span of time.

Example for a 15-minute speech:

Intro	= Could be 3 minutes—may be about yourself and start of talk
Second part	= Starts at 3-minute mark—you may have the main part of your talk
Third part	= Start at 6-minute mark—you may want to interact with the audience
Outro	= Could be 3 minutes before the end, where you give a summary of your talk and wrap up. Or even answer questions sent in earlier.

WORKING WITH A VARIETY OF REPERTOIRE

Many vocal artists in the past had sung and stuck to a particular style of singing. In most cases, I would relate this to the saying, "If it ain't broke don't fix it." Because those who stuck to a particular genre were doing so well that there was no real point in doing different genres or repertoire. For example, an established vocalist like the late Luther Vandross was known for ballads, and he rocked them. Also, many people invested in him. So, it worked for him to stay within that genre of music.

Although, if someone came to me as a newbie, I would encourage them to work on different genres of music. I would not want them to be a one-trick pony as it limits their ability, scope, and opportunities. I work with clients to coach them on how to use their voices rather than perform one specific genre.

SPEAKERS

I have always recommended speakers to go online and listen to other speakers and realise who their favourites are. Then think about why, take the parts that appeal to them, and see how they can incorporate these good parts into their presentations, just as I would recommend my singing students to listen to different artists. You must observe your favourite speaker as they discuss different subjects as well as different speakers who may be speaking about the same topics. This is not just to widen the subjects the students can speak about. It is also to learn from other speakers what they could put into their personal speeches.

PERFORMANCE

I realised that performance is something people generally do all the time. Now when one performs and messes up in everyday life, it does not feel as bad as when you are on stage. Because so many more people see you when you are in the limelight. So, I saw it fit to work on the following areas to top off the pre-sentation/recital process.

DELIVERY, STAGE PRESENCE, MIC TECHNIQUES

Not paying attention to the above could cost you to lose your opportunities to perform or present at other venues.

The following is how the delivery, mic techniques, and stage presence can impact your performance:

- *Vocal delivery* includes components of speech delivery that relate to your voice and, thus, your performance. These can include but are not limited to volume, pitch, articulation, pronunciation, and fluency. Our voice is important to consider when delivering our song or speech for two main reasons. First, vocal delivery can help us engage and interest the audience. Secondly, it helps our audience understand our perfor-mance and have a more meaningful experience.
- *Your stage presence* is about feeling free and vulnerable while you tell your story. When your mind is opened to this, you connect with the audience, and they can visualise, feel, and join you on your vocal journey.
  - Develop an image that portrays who you are or want to be. Make sure that you consider your performance venue because you do not want to turn up to a gig where they are serving a 5-course meal in a 5-star hotel where people are paying £500 per plate, and you are rocking the Goth look, with your black and torn fishnet stockings or ripped jeans.
  - Try not to move around the stage too much if you do not have your breathing to a place where it will complement and enhance

the sounds you want to produce and the notes you want to hit and/or hold.

- Make a connection with the audience wherever you can if you can see off the stage—as sometimes the lighting prevents this possibility. If they are blocked from your sight, pretend you are singing to someone and present your piece with a passion. According to Yvonne Caruthers, "Charisma is not something which can be added to make a performance better; it exists because a performer believes strongly in what s/he is doing." So, if you know your song well, as shown in the breaking down the song section, you should be very convincing.

+ *Mic techniques* require you to be there for your mic check when performing. Be confident enough to let the sound engineer know when you cannot hear yourself clearly, and do not stop until you do hear yourself with clarity in your stage monitors. Plus, know your song to the point that if you are going to belt or hit a high note, you pull the mic away from your mouth, as this can be very hurtful to the audience's ear.

Also, use a mic like a toothbrush but do not place it in your mouth. If you think about the number of people that have used the mic before you, you will understand my advice.

HARMONY

For those of you that work in choirs or groups where reading music is a requirement, and you only achieve harmony by singing what is written, then what I am about to explain may not apply to you. This will be helpful for those who do not read music and rely on the ear to achieve harmony. You must work with someone who sings in tune and is competent in singing and holding a note or vocalizing all parts of melodies to songs you are working on. The basics of harmony are that a person sings a note, and then you sing a third above or below that note. The beauty of practicing scales, arpeggios, or whatever your choice of vocal exercise may be, is that you will begin to feel when a note is off. This will cause you to shift your note to a more accurate place and thus create a harmonic sound.

Additionally, a kind word of advice, if you are going to perform a song where harmonies are required for it to sound on point (if you are not already a professional, do this every day), it is important that you practice with the persons you are singing with as frequently as is humanly possible. My reason for stressing that is not just that harmony sounds awful when a person is not on their correct note, but it can also be the reason an event organiser crosses you off their list of future performers. Our voice coach from Aria School of Voice always stressed, "You are as good as your weakest link and/or your last performance." So, no matter how great you were at your previous appearances, if the last one was a flop, that is what people will remember.

For those who read music, the above example is self-explanatory. But for those who do not, I want to stress that you are blessed if you have four singers for all four notes to work with. This is not a major issue if you keep all your notes a third apart.

Do Re **Me** Fa **Sol** La Ti **Do** is your scale, but when you want to harmonise, you will only be interested in the notes that are in bold and notice that these are the notes of the arpeggio.

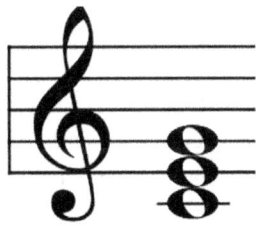

The above is a C chord, which creates harmony when sung simultaneously, plus, when you add the Doh (C) above from the next octave, you create an even fuller sound.

Harmony is not just important for stage performances but also came in handy in my life too. As I grew in my life, I believed the people in my circle who kept telling me that I was too sensitive, I took things too personally, and that they had to think carefully before they spoke to me. I started thinking I was too full on as I adapted to speaking my truth to those people. I realised I felt the sensitivity because these people were not in harmony with how my life was supposed to flow. When I began to voice my truth and stand firm in it, I could see how my life was becoming calm, content, and surrounded by genuine and loving people, and so many more loving things were happening. I could then see that living in harmony could only be created by being around the right people. Similarly, only the right notes could create a beautiful harmonic sound.

VOICE CARE

Recognise that as singers, our body is our instrument. So, for this reason, we must take care of it. Here are some suggestions I have picked up along my vocal journey that have helped me along the way. Please note that I have been in situations where all these things have not always been possible, so just do your best to protect and take care of your body and, thus, your vocals.

1. When you are due to perform, warm up your vocals before performances.
2. Try and have some rest days before performance day also.
3. If you cannot take days off work, then at least clear your schedule for the whole performance day, even if it is scheduled in the evening. Remember, your body is your instrument.
4. Cow's milk in any form, including chocolate, should be avoided, specifically on performance days. This, plus black currant drinks, tend to create phlegm in the throat, which causes you to keep coughing, causing a disruptive performance in some cases. Remember, every person's body reacts differently to different things.
5. I would advise you to stop smoking, as in some cases, it can cause havoc and even speed up the deterioration of your vocal cords. We

place strain on our vocals to finish the song, which leaves us sore in the long run.

6. I understand that many of you are also drinkers of alcohol but be advised that it is dehydrating and can also be inflammatory. So, I advise you to avoid, lessen the amount, or even better, give up both if you want your voice to be healthier.

7. My number one recommendation for the vocalist is water but loading yourself with water on the day of the performance is not enough. Get into the habit of keeping the vocals hydrated by drinking the amount of water that is good for your weight daily. The best way for singers or speakers to drink water is to have it at room temperature, as our bodies and vocals do not react well to iced or hot water. Some singers drink lemon and honey in warm water around the time of rehearsals and performances. This is a good habit too. Herbal decaffeinated teas are also a good option when you want a break from the water, as caffeinated drinks are said to alter your sound even though studies are still being done.

Although you are looking at the care of your voice, which requires self-care, too, I have found that it has motivated the women I have worked with to improve other areas of their lives.

DRAMA

Start looking at your song or your speech as a mini-movie. They all have a beginning, a middle, and an end. Another way of looking at this aspect of performance is that you are acting out the song or speech instead of dramatizing the scene. One of the examples I would give my students is to picture themselves at a wedding, singing a song about love and happiness, yet they are sad and pouty, looking like they want to cry from unhappiness. This would not be an effective way to express this song, so your best way is to look at the performer and how they expressed or portrayed the song. Then look at what the song means to you and how you would like to portray that song. Remember that if you are singing to a large audience, everyone will interpret your rendition of the song in their way, so just focus on making the song yours. Look at other performers or speakers to get some other performance ideas for your recital or speech.

YOUR BODY—FITNESS

I am not saying to hit the gym every day and go on a crazy diet that makes you cranky. I have learnt enough in my life to know that deprivation diets and going to the gym daily are not necessarily the best way to lose weight. It is in the food you eat. I am suggesting that you look at companies that suggest you should do less exercise and eat better. If you are puffing and panting just to walk up and down the stairs at home, then start looking at what you can do to change that. There is a good chance that you need to do something different for your body to function better.

When I was in Aria School of Voice, I remember running up and down steps for stamina and conditioning, doing exercises to tighten the lower stomach muscles, and of course, vocal exercises too. That was all good when I was younger, but I have discovered that you do not need to be half that rigorous if you eat the right foods for your body. Therefore, I am suggesting you take some time out, prepare great healthy food, and find short, sharp bursts of movements that do not require you to do hours of exercise per day. Or just walk each day; you will be amazed at how much that helps.

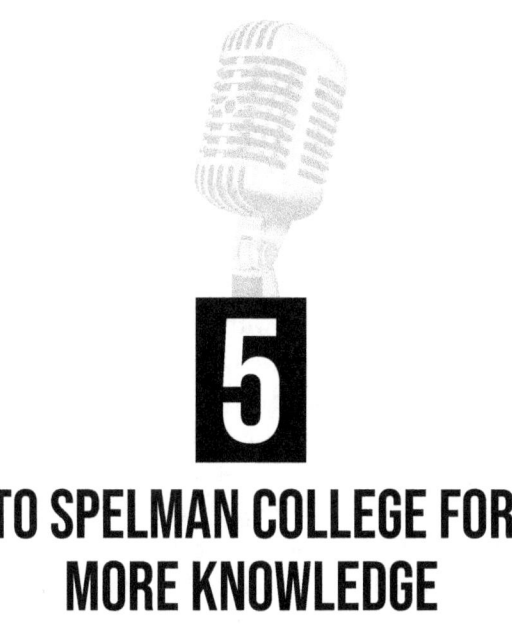

5

TO SPELMAN COLLEGE FOR MORE KNOWLEDGE

My drive to make sure my clients got the best out of their area and took courage
So off To Spelman college, I went to gain more knowledge

A major goal or dream of mine was always to live in the USA at some time in my life. As a kid, whenever I saw a Black person on TV, it always seemed to be a film or series from America, so being an entertainer, I thought that must be the place to go. Plus, it made me see the possibility of being on television. So determined was I to make it across the pond to the US that I decided to reawaken this dream, which lay dormant for most of my life. Although I had not learnt about the depth and real possibilities of setting goals, I would sit and write them out on the first of January of each year. Five years before moving to the USA, I added this dream of living in the USA to my annual list of goals. In 2003, it was suggested on three separate occasions that Spelman College was the place to attend if I was considering studying abroad.

An ex-vocal student of mine invited me to see a musical with her and her family, some of whom were visiting from the USA. They were going to see the musical UMOJA in London, and I gladly accepted the invitation. We all had such an awesome time that I was invited out again, but it was to go Salsa dancing this time. There was more space to speak to her visiting family on this occasion. Our conversation quickly shifted to the fact that I had always wanted to live in the USA at some stage and how I had found out that being a student was the most legitimate way to do so. Straight away, her uncle told me that if I was going to the USA, I should go to Spelman College. Although I heard what he said, I did not pay much attention.

Plus, my sons used to play out with another boy in my neighbourhood whose father came to my home one day looking for him. When I heard his American accent, I started speaking about my dream to get to America on a student visa. Again, his first suggestion and statement were, "If you want to study over there, you have to attend Spelman College." After having heard it for the second time, I was intrigued enough to go and find out what this school looked like. So, I went to their website to see if I could get a feeling of what this institution was about and if I felt a connection. Unfortunately, I had learnt from my home country that anything all black was not a positive thing. Additionally, my grandmother had taught me that it was better to have one girlfriend and ninety-nine boyfriends than vice versa. Therefore, as this college was an all-black, all-female one, I dismissed it immediately.

Fortunately, this was not where my signs stopped. I was given a further sign from a company called FastWeb where I had registered for help through this school searching procedure. I joined this site because it not only took my infor-mation and suggested specific schools that may be great for my character, but it also showed places where I could apply for funding towards my schooling. Those scholarships and grants were suggested based on the types of education you had achieved or if you or your family members were affiliated with any specific employers. I was minding my own business when I received a message from this website stating that Spelman College would love someone like me to attend their institution. As you can imagine, three signs were enough to know that the Almighty was guiding me to apply to this college. Hence, I found their contact information and connected to the appropriate department that would confirm what papers I needed to get together, what qualifications I needed, and how much of my education could be transferred to my degree. I looked at their Music Department and decided on the path I would take during this part of my journey.

Faith was always a strong point in my life; with that, I felt so deeply about my signs and what was about to unfold. So, I decided to take a trip to Atlanta (ATL), Georgia, to get a feel of the area and, of course, Spelman College.

Subsequently, I invited a girlfriend of mine and her daughter to join my two sons and me to check out ATL. The Uncle of my ex-student offered to put us up for one week, and we spent the other week at Disney Land Orlando to give the children a great holiday. During my time in ATL, I managed to visit Spelman for two days and loved the warmth I felt. I did not realise until then how literally being surrounded by students of my colour could make me feel warm, happy, and connected. I met with the head of the department for mature students, and she declared that I did not have as rigid an application process as the traditional students. You can only imagine what music that was to my ears. On top of that, she arranged for me to meet a few members of staff and faculty that she felt would be of benefit to me. I decided that until I knew where I would live, I did not need to get a feel of any specific area. We checked out a few local restaurants, a jazz club called Sambuca, and malls to go shopping. We then hired a car and drove down to Orlando, where we had a wonderful week with our children.

While in Atlanta, I remember the International Advisor letting me know the yearly cost of tuition and fees but not being phased by the amount. I just knew that I was going to be a student here. It was interesting that during the year 2004, I started doing things like clearing out my loft. I looked for money in all the places I was directed to, including UCAS and Fulbright. I researched scholarships here in the UK to possibly fund my studies in the US, but nothing appeared. I guess that there were not many systems that wanted to invest in someone of my age. Though, I did not let the negative responses stop me from preparing for the next step, which was to let the college know that I had the funds and to send the proof. Two young people were not as enthusiastic as I was, though.

My two children were very concerned and needed a decision on whether we were going to the USA or not. They did not want to leave their friends, and I remember that my oldest was concerned that he had been offered a place at a school where he would be with many of his friends. For that reason, he did not want to leave the UK, so I took a leap of faith and gave my children the random date of Wednesday, 15th of June 2004. I promised them that if, by this date, God had not shown me the funding to at least start this venture, then I was going to forfeit this dream and stay here in the UK.

I decided to apply to Spelman College as a Vocal Performance Major because vocal artistry was always my passion, whether I performed, studied,

41

or taught it. So as this was the course that would give me more knowledge and practical experience about my subject, this is what I pursued. The main thing that caused doubts about getting into this college was money because I could not live on campus at the time due to having children. Moreover, I was thinking about the possibility of money not turning up on time for me to start in August. There were also some concerns about what my Plan B would be if things did not work out. I could ask my uncle to stay in my UK home, but what would I do if he chose not to? I decided to leave that again to the Almighty. The other concern was whether I would be accepted into my chosen course. I say all that to say that it was not 100% positive and light throughout this entire process. Nonetheless, concerns or not, I kept pushing through as I have always done.

As the date grew closer, I asked God to show me a sign. Plus, I was calmly preparing things that I felt I needed to do before I had to change gears and start focusing on the necessities to get to the USA. On the morning of Wednesday, the 15th of June 2004, I received a loan application through my front door. I remember looking at the envelope and thinking, could this possibly be what I have been waiting for? I picked it up, and by then, my breathing had grown intense, and my heart felt like it was beating out of my chest. I opened the letter to find that it was a loan application for the exact amount I needed. I recall looking at the form and seeing the different amounts I could apply for. I looked at the largest amount and had to check myself. In my thoughts, I was wondering whether they would give me such a large amount instead of looking into my heart and applying for what I needed to pursue this part of my life. All this was going on while I paced up and down in my kitchen, telling myself that, as I was on this date, surely it was too late to do anything now instead of realizing that I had asked and named the date when I wanted a reply. Now that it was here, I debated with myself instead of receiving what I asked for. Subsequently, I went up to my bedroom while trying to calm my heartbeat down and made the phone call to the bank. When she said to wait while she checked the outcome of my application, I was not sure how I managed not to hyperventilate. She then responded by letting me know that they were going to give me the loan, and this was where my head nearly exploded. I flew off the chair; if I had been taller, my head would probably have hit the ceiling. I believe I called Spelman College that day to find out what I needed to do next.

After that previous experience, I knew that an extreme amount of faith and tenacity would be needed to overcome the obstacles to get through this phase of my life. I say this because not only did my adversaries seem unsurmountable, but I still feel that I underestimated the magnitude of many of my challenges. To start with, I did not realise how much more I needed to do in addition to proving my financial status, thus shortening the time I had to pack my things to leave.

VISA APPLICATION PROCESS DURING 2004

First, I had to send copies of my certificates so that the college could verify any transferable credits after allowing me to clarify and give information about things that were not as straightforward as they appeared. The non-traditional students' department Pauline E. Drake Students (PEDS) informed the International Advisor (IA) that all was well with my paperwork. I sent the application and its fee, plus proof of finances to take care of my children and me, to Spelman to get hold of the paperwork needed for my visa interview. There was so much I needed to complete that I was beginning to think it might not have happened that year. I waited in anticipation for the IA's response and the I20 document and was ready to go, regardless of the time constraints.

Applying for visas was the first and most crucial step I had to take, and with only six weeks to go until I was supposed to be at the college for the induction, things got very overwhelming. I would like to emphasise here to be very careful who you keep in your friends and family circle. As I realised that although their negative words can build your character, those same words can crush your dreams and hinder your progress. I share this because so many of my friends and family at the time told me how impossible it would be to get a visa in such a short time.

VISA PROCESS AT THE TIME

So, as I have always done and always will do, I put my faith in the Almighty and went online, filled out, downloaded, and printed the visa application forms.

I then took those forms to my local post office and paid the fees. With my payment, it was shown at the American Embassy that I was official, and I also had a number that I guess could be used to track me while living in the USA.

I then called the American Embassy and booked my interview for the following Thursday of the week after payment.

The day of the interview came, and I have to say that the only reason I was nervous while waiting to be seen was again due to the stories others told me. I was told to make sure I kept my mouth shut unless to directly answer the questions asked. I remember walking up to a cubicle in the American Embassy, and my heart was pounding out of my mouth. Although by now I knew deep in my heart this was meant to be, I still had the negatives swirling around in my head, and of course, it was nothing like the adverse experience people had told me to expect. I was asked three questions, and the interviewer behind the counter just told me all was well. She asked me why I chose the USA, and I took pride in responding to her question. So, after all that stress, I received all three visas in our passports by the following Friday morning—so much for not being able to do this in six weeks.

THINGS I HAD TO TAKE CARE OF BEFORE DEPARTURE

I had to make sure my uncle could stay in my home, and to accomplish this, I made a list of what he would have to take care of and what he needed to pay for, such as bills, rent, council tax, etc. Because he was okay with this, it meant one less stress to deal with once I was away. It was essential to have someone stay instead of just giving up my home. As I was a single mum who was going to a foreign country, where I only knew the family that was going to house me until I got on my feet, I wanted the security of knowing that if I should return, then we would not be homeless.

As part of my preparation for accepting the offer at Spelman College, you probably remember that a friend, my sons, and I visited my ex-student's uncle. Well, while we were there, his wife offered for us to stay at their home until we worked things out for our long-term stay if I was accepted. Now, this was very comforting and exciting to know that someone would do this for us, so I gladly accepted her offer. I did not expect what happened, which put me in a very sinister position. I tried calling her for at least four weeks before leaving because I had given her my travel dates and wanted to ensure all was well with what we had previously agreed on. I called her constantly, close to our departure, to confirm that arrangements still stood. I received a call back on

Wednesday evening, two days before we flew. She explained that she could no longer accommodate us as she and her husband were both working that weekend. I was overcome with fear when I put that phone down. Thinking, what could I do at such short notice? I spoke to a positive girlfriend who advised me on what she thought I should do, and I followed that advice and went ahead with my plan to leave. I arranged for an apartment search with REMAX, the property service, with a plan to get a taxi from the airport to a hotel local to their branch to view apartments on Saturday.

The six-week part of my journey was the most stressful. I seemed to have had everything in place except packing to leave. Being up until at least 3:00 AM Friday packing for departure in the few hours that followed, my uncle tried to calm me down by offering to release some of the pressure of things I was yet to handle. Making sure the boys were sorted, their hand luggage was packed, and everything else was done in time for departure reduced me to tears, and I was in a state of hysterics. I could not see a way forward. I guess I was so focused on what more could go wrong I was not thinking about how much I had already achieved. I managed to get to the airport on time and proudly travelled on Friday, the 13th of August. I say proudly because many people questioned why Friday the 13th (unlucky for some). It was because I got 50% off our flights, plus I was not superstitious.

The family we were to stay with ended up accommodating us after all. Fortunately, my ex-student's uncle, who we all called Uncle Syl, had taken time off work to help us over that weekend. Noting that this family was very busy was experience enough to realise, at least in my head, that I needed to sort myself and my sons out as soon as possible. So, this is how the first week went. We chilled on Friday when we got to their home. On Saturday, Uncle Syl took us on the property search. I saw an apartment I liked and filled out the required paperwork. On Sunday, he took us to view cars, and I found one I liked and purchased that. On Monday, I found a clinic to get the boys further vaccinations for school and then went and registered them. Plus, the property accepted my application on this day too. On Tuesday, my youngest son started school, which was nerve-racking, and we moved into the apartment that evening. On Wednesday, my oldest son started school, and I also went and purchased furniture for the apartment. On Thursday, the furniture was delivered and set up for me, and I went to college while the boys were at school on Friday. What a week! Experiences like these confirm to me that I am blessed and highly favoured.

6

FROM SPELMAN COLLEGE GLEE CLUB TO THE JAZZ ENSEMBLE

From Spelman college Glee Club to the Jazz Ensemble
I fought, grew, and stumbled, making sure this was made possible

onsidering this was an all-black Women's College, I grew tired of the nearly 100% classical music we would perform in the Glee Club. Yes, of course, it was an amazing experience when we performed, but because most of my vocal lessons involved performing classical music as well, it became a bit much. I was under the impression that being a member of The Spelman Jazz Ensemble was not an option. The Chair of the department led me to believe that if you were a performance major, which I was then, I had to be in the Glee Club. The hours that we did between rehearsals, sectionals, and performances meant that I could not possibly fit in the Jazz Ensemble as well. I was later informed that I could be in any ensemble I wanted and set about making the swap, a mission of mine.

At this stage in my life, I was still speaking very quietly when there was any doubt about whether I would get what I needed, and I still held quite a strong fear of rejection. Again, I wanted to be heard, so I spoke up to get myself out of the Glee Club. My first approach was to the Director of the Jazz Ensemble, who confirmed that I could be a member if I auditioned. My Chair not only asked me who gave me the right to audition but also asked me to put into writing why I felt I should be permitted to do this. I asked a professor of mine to proofread the letter, and when she started reading it, she asked me why it was even being written. After explaining, she advised me to take this matter to the Dean as this was not necessary or right. Feeling a little nervous, I took it to the Dean as advised. They listened to the fact that I had filled out an add/drop slip and had been told that I would not get a signature to make this happen. So, they arranged another meeting among themselves and told me that if the Chair would not sign the slip, they would if this was necessary.

I joined the Jazz Ensemble in my third year at Spelman and loved it. I had not felt so elated in a singing space for a long time. I knew it was the right decision. I was so ready for this awesome change that I took on as many roles as I could manage. My primary role was that of a vocal artist in the actual ensemble. I enjoyed being the secretary because apart from photocopying and ensuring everyone had their sheet music, I coordinated the information they needed for their schedules, including locations and event times. I have to say this role took my growth from where I was in life to another level. I had to manage all the members' college schedules and those of the ensemble. I set up times for rehearsals and photoshoots and scheduled meetings with them at certain stores so we could buy suits for our spring tours. I researched quotes for coaches and hotels for our future tours and designed logos for the jackets we wore to our performances. I also worked on sectionals with the vocalists whenever I was needed and tried to keep a check on the Ensemble members whenever possible while we were on tour. Even though some of the girls did not appreciate me trying to keep them on track, some missed me keeping them in line when I left. I guess I played an important role for some of the members.

Music Theory always gave me a challenge. As a result, the Chair of the Department gave me an ultimatum. This was that I either had to start a new major or do two more years of music. At Spelman, you could not get below a C in a core subject which I received in the subject of Music Theory. As this was happening, I feared that I had come to the states to achieve a Music Performance BA, which could be swatted due to a particular course in the major. Many students who respected and supported me urged me to visit the Women's Study Department. I thought nothing ventured, nothing gained. I visited with Dr. Kuumba, a professor who managed me in starting a new BA, which I completed at the same time as my Music Performance peers. She transferred some of my high-level courses and created a music concentration degree. Consequently, I managed to start a new degree geared towards music while completing a Comparative Woman Studies BA and a Music minor.

WHAT STOOD OUT FOR ME IN MY LEARNING ABOUT POWERFUL WOMEN (IN MY COMPARATIVE WOMEN STUDIES DEGREE)

The fact that these women did so many things that people just do not know about is no longer a surprise for me. Here are a few examples:

A group of illiterate African women brought Mobil Oil Company to its knees after the company decided that they would dump their waste in nearby waters, which were harmful to these women and their people.

In earlier times, African countries had black female rulers in authority that counselled the villagers and were approached for advice on how to run their countries.

There were and still are female African Presidents I was unaware of at the time. I recognise the extremes the system will go through to conceal this information, which still makes me sad.

I did my final paper on female Rastafarians in Reggae music and what they were up against.

Even though Rastas were and may still be very patriarchal, their roots stem from what was thought to be the Nyabinghi culture. It turns out that the name came from Queen Nyabinghi, who turned out to be a revered goddess.

The I-Threes, Bob Marley's backing singers, signed away most of their rights to many of the songs they co-produced.

They even wrote and produced tracks where their ownership was stolen, and thus money was taken away from them. They were looked upon as voices rather than human beings and had to fight for what little they did receive.

The I-Threes took their experiences within the music industry for Bob Marley and used them to educate other women who may have been suffering the same kind of misogynistic treatment.

Before going to the USA, I had told myself that I wanted a community in which to worship God, and I went in search of my spiritual home in the UK. Unfortunately, I did not find one for two main reasons that kept coming up in nearly all the churches I visited. The first reason was that the service seemed to end at least two hours after the scheduled end time. The second reason was the Sunday School teachers never wanted to let me in their classrooms to at least ease my sons into being alone with strangers. Going by the new things I was learning about history compared to what was being taught in the churches, it was important to me to know what was being taught in their classes. I concluded that I did not need four walls to be able to have a relationship with God, so I just kept Her close to my heart and continued my 15 minutes per day of meditation to keep checking in with Her.

I remember being on campus and mentioning the previous encounters to my Spelman sister. While I told her about my search, she just said, "You will love the Bahai faith." This was stated and accepted by me quite organically. We kept on talking, and she said nothing more. Less than a month later, another Spelman sister visited the same Bahai Centre close to my home. She came from her visit raving about how this was the perfect place for my spiritual home. As I respected my friend's word, I visited the Bahai Centre the next week. I remember vividly that as soon as I opened the doors, the love that hit me let me know that this was where I would commune with God, and I have been a member ever since. I loved the energy, people, and principles, so I signed up as soon as possible. I also remember enjoying the choir so much and voicing that I would love to be a member. A Bahai member said, "Well, if that is what you want, then go and join them," and I did. There was a little hesitation, as I recalled most churches did not allow you to join in their activities unless you were a legitimate member worshipping in the same way they did.

I started feeling a little nervous when my body showed signs of being pregnant. It was the semester before I was due to graduate that it was confirmed. I went for a pregnancy test on three separate occasions. First, I went to the college hospital, and they told me the test was positive. Then I went to a private clinic, and the third test was done in the county clinic. As each one of these institutions gave me the exact same due date, I had to accept that this was happening. This came as a big shock to me, as I felt I was far too old to be having a baby, and besides, I thought my pregnancy days were over. So, as the phrase goes, I had to put my big girl panties on even though the morning sickness was the worst ever and keep my life moving. Not only did I know I would keep this baby, but I also knew I would graduate. Quitting was never my forte, and I was not about to start now, especially when it came to major things like these. I told the boys the news, and when I look back, it is funny how shocked they were.

They made me feel like a dinosaur as their response showed me that I had no business having intimate relations with anyone. I felt sad that the father of my child was not too keen on me but felt happy that he was very excited about the baby. I was also unprepared for the adverse challenges I was about to embark upon. However, I can proudly say I went through them and am here to tell the story.

I had difficulty finding employment shortly after having my daughter and ended up calling my International Advisor to see if she could help. She was shocked that I was still in the USA and explained that I should have gone home already. She added that if I overstayed my visa's end date, December 31st of that year, I could get a 10-year ban from returning to the US. Upon reflection on what she told me, the pros of going home outweighed the cons. Plus, it was not working out well with my daughter's father, so I willingly packed up to go home.

I understood that the first five years were one of the most important times in a child's life, and I knew I could stay home with her back in the UK. So, I gracefully accepted closure to this chapter of my life and flew home in November of the same year I graduated. I had gotten over the fact that I would be seen as a failure by returning to the UK, and I started to put plans into place to leave the USA. I felt deflated because my goal was to graduate, get a great job, and enjoy a life of opportunities that would have me in a great space. I did not feel warmly received by my family, but again I was warned at the start of this degree. I returned to an empty house that was fully furnished when I left. Consequently, I had to start over as I did when I arrived in Atlanta. I had a beautiful new baby daughter and two sons that would positively distract me from what was happening in my world, and I was grateful for this.

7

MAKING A BUSINESS OF MA GAINED AT TEXAS WOMAN'S UNIVERSITY

Making a business using the MA gained at Texas Woman's University
Working with the kids through the summer gave me clarity

SECOND TIME AROUND

I graduated with an MA in Education in Teaching, Learning, and Curriculum in December 2017. I postponed my actual graduation ceremony to the following year, hoping more people could attend. Unfortunately, only two people outside my daughter made it to my graduation: my paternal uncle and my awesome friend I met soon after arriving in Texas. I had mixed feelings about this fact, including being sad, humbled, excited, elated, relieved, grateful, unappreciated for my achievement, proud of myself, and thankful that it was all over.

Although it took me close to 10 years to work out how to plan, schedule, and author a paper so that I could give it in early instead of stressing about a deadline. For my final paper, this goal was accomplished. I guess part of it was that I was not juggling so many hats at the completion time. There were many thoughts about what I would do next. For that time, I continued as a facilitator for Grade 4 children on their history trips. I did not want to do this as a full-time career, as music was always my passion, although I still needed to earn some money. I needed more money than I was making, so while at a job fair, I was recruited to the above job, and to be honest, although standing for much of my day was a killer on the feet, I thoroughly enjoyed the interaction with the kids.

I held a Graduate Assistant position for at least two years that finished at the end of the spring semester. Therefore, I started speaking to many people about wanting to start a voice coaching business in the summer of 2016. While placing my energy out there, in walked Mel, who I could only have described as a Godsend at the time. She was a parent I had met at my daughter's school. She pushed me toward getting things started, even though it was only a few weeks until the start of the summer break. She loved graphics, so I sent her my idea for a logo. She put her spin on it and created a flyer which I distributed widely. I tweaked the original flyer to adapt to the different age groups and went ahead with the start date.

Mel used to send her son to a nursery that she remembered stayed closed during the summer. She encouraged me to enquire about availability for a few weeks. I found out that it was available for me to hire during the summer. Since the venue was a nursery, it was a very young environment. This was great for the young children but not the older ones. Mel gave me the idea of setting up workshops for different age groups so that I could reach out to more students and therefore make more of an income. Fortunately, the nursery agreed to rent me their space for three weeks in the summer because they knew Mel. Consequently, I went about putting formal parts of the business in place, such as registering it, opening a business bank account, and getting liability insurance. Then I researched and proceeded to set up an online payment system, which prevented me from having to take individual fees. In addition, I contacted my daughter's ballet schoolteacher and asked if I could rent her space for my older students, which was also approved.

SETTING UP FOR THE 3.5 TO 7.5-YEAR-OLD VOCAL WORKSHOP

Setting up a voice workshop for 3.5 to 8-year-olds required me to extract small exercises from my curriculum and include nursery rhymes, plus arts and crafts. I decided on a big song that would be acted out at the end of their week. And, for that song, we all would have created a mask to go with that song during our arts and crafts sessions. As the students for this age group all turned out to be 3.5 to 4-year-olds, we mainly sang nursery rhymes and did fun solfege exercises. This was an enjoyable experience because I was more accustomed to working with larger-sized groups that were this age, which allowed them to work with each other. As these parents found out so late, there were only a few in these classes, which meant I had to have my creativity hat on, firm and strong. This also allowed a bond I did not get with larger groups, so I loved this.

SETTING UP FOR THE 8 TO 15-YEAR-OLD VOCAL WORKSHOP

Once again, I extracted lessons from my curriculum. The students worked on songs they loved to sing, plus I included meditation, and they performed a show at the end of the week for their friends and family. My daughter's ballet school venue turned out to be the perfect venue for the show, and it was great to see the students do so well in less than 2 weeks. This was a learning experience that helped diminish my doubts about teaching meditation to young students. To watch them get excited about meditating was awesome. I started them off at 10 seconds, I believe, and increased it by 10 seconds daily, only to find that they wanted to increase the time even more by the third day. They enjoyed the calm they got out of this exercise. I enjoyed their amazement at recognizing more instruments and what was going on in their songs which they had never paid attention to before. They enjoyed learning new things outside the musical box of songs they had become accustomed to listening to on most occasions. They could now see the benefits and the limitations they placed on themselves by only listening to and performing one genre of music and nothing else.

CHALLENGES WITH CHILDCARE

The hours I intended to do for these voice camps meant that my daughter was attending summer school camp most of the time. And as she had so many problems at school, specifically with bullies, I feared leaving her with a new set of people. She managed to settle well at the MLK center and came out bully-free. My fear slowed down my movements a little because, in the back of my mind, I did not want or need her to meet a new set of bullies. The lesson here is that sometimes you must let fear go and let God take over.

VOLUNTEERING YOUR SERVICES AND WORKING YOUR INSTRUMENT

Performing for my University wherever and whenever requested was something I found helpful for keeping my eclectic vocal abilities alive. Plus, I recognised that the musical works we had to study, listen to, and perform were all very classically oriented. To allow me to express myself on a broader range than they offered, I found it necessary to volunteer so I could perform songs I preferred.

Volunteering to work with voices in the summer of 2018 was also an awesome experience that was very fulfilling. Working with children, whether infants or teenagers, have always been the most rewarding time of my teaching. It is because they have very few inhibitions, and I can work at my best when fear is not in the way of the student. Without that element of fear, they do the exercises I give them to get the desired results. With adults, although not all of them, we carry so much baggage that there is usually a reason why what I am giving them may not work and take longer to move forward. This part of my work took place in a Bahai summer program which I was asked to teach by a Bahai Sister who believed in my vocal and teaching ability. Our word for that summer was 'Integrity,' and it was for us to come up with a song. During their other sessions, they came up with an acronym for the word "Integrity." We used this and the backing track to a popular song they all knew and enjoyed. We chose the song from a list of their favourite songs that I requested them to compile. We listened to a snippet of the songs that I did not know, and I decided on which ones we would put to a vote. We then ended up voting on the ones whose words were appropriate and used the song with the most votes. Then I arranged the word "Integrity" to fit into the chorus and the acronym to fit into the verses.

ALSO PAID WORK

I ended up teaching Special Educational Needs (SEN) students without even knowing this was the case. The blessed woman I was living with at the end of my stay in Texas suggested I call someone she knew that owned a music school. So, I enquired to see if she had any vocal work, and it turned out that this woman did. My new employer intentionally did not tell me that her clients were SEN students. This took away the doubt I may have had should I have known. Fortunately for her, I never judged students according to their abilities. I have always held and still hold high expectations of the students I teach and put out positive energy with the intention that they will produce what I ask of them rather than think about whether they can do the exercise or not. Then I would plan my lessons to take them from wherever they were.

1st soprano for the catholic church

Near my departure from the US, I found out that a local choir director was auditioning for some vocalists. I decided to apply and got a position as 2nd Soprano and ended up doing 1st soprano. As he did not ask me to prepare a particular song, I chose the one I was extremely comfortable with and got in as 1st soprano. I have to say that within the time spent here, I decided I was blessed in so many ways. One of those was that the woman I sang next to turned out to live about five minutes away from me. This meant I did not have to burden the woman who housed me with having to get me to church every Sunday at 7:30 am. Plus, the singer colleague from the choir was also able to drive me home on Wednesday evenings, so everything worked out well. Now, all was taken care of while doing what I loved, singing.

Subbing for a School District

Mansfield county, where I also subbed toward the end of my stay in the United States, did not allow me to work for any other county while working for them. Becoming employed by them was a very long and tedious process. Although, I followed it through because I realised it was the step in the door I needed to get into future classrooms. I also needed a way to care for myself and my daughter financially. It was a very stressful time because much negativity was going on while I was trying to work. I intended to apply for all the musical subbing jobs to keep working in my field, but unfortunately, it did not work out that way. I was not in a position to decline the job opportunities solely because they were not my first choice. So, I went ahead and took the other jobs, which were so structured there was no way I could fail. I soon discovered the age groups I was happy with and stuck to those.

GIVING UP OUR HOME, AGAIN

With literally zero income being received, I had to make the devasting decision to uproot my daughter, give up our property, and move again. It was no longer an option to stay where we were; I moved us out before we were forced out. Where we were going to stay was so last minute.com that I had decided to go live with a woman I barely knew. She was my cousin's mother and ex-wife to my uncle, and I should have known this was not the right decision, but we needed somewhere to live. Fortunately for me, I was given a red flag by God on the night I was leaving to go to her home that this was not the right place for us. She left a message with her daughter saying she did not want us in her home when we had our removal van packed up to leave at about 10:30 pm. She changed her mind that night because she was making it very clear that if she could not discipline my daughter in the way she wanted, then there would be a problem. Plus, she told me that my child and I could not wear trousers while we were in her house. We could do what we wanted outside but not inside. I called my uncle and let him know the situation and drove to his home and unloaded my possessions into his garage instead. I took the van back to the storage place, and we probably got home at around 2 am the following day. God also blessed me with someone who offered us an alternative accommodation, should I need it.

While I was still in my apartment packing up, I happened to be speaking to a friend about my situation, who told me her home was an option if I did not find somewhere to live. After spending a very short time with my uncle, I decided to take her up on her offer only to regret this decision. I ended up living with a woman whose behaviours were unacceptable to me. The environment I ended up in was not somewhere I could stay long-term. I found this out very soon after my arrival. She watched my every move. She attended many networking meetings and had a problem if I did not join her. Then, when we were out at these meetings, she proudly told everyone that she was housing me, which I found very uncomfortable. I also found myself cleaning up after everyone as if I were the hired help. The environment got so toxic that I had to leave.

Finally, I ended up in a home full of love and support—at least from the owners. When I went to their home and told them my predicament, the intention was to be able to bring my stuff to their home while I sought refuge at a woman's shelter. Luckily, it did not work that way. My Bahai sister was not having me live that life and allowed me to sleep on her sofa. I explained my situation, and she allowed me to stay until her other family moved out. I am unsure if she realised it, but this awesome woman became one of the many mothers I never had. I could talk to her about anything as she was empathic, supportive, a good listener, and a great encourager. Whatever my need, if it were within her capacity, she would always help.

8

UNDERSTANDING THAT I SPOKE THROUGH SINGING—THERAPY/COUNSELLING

That in my world, there will always be children, teaching and singing
Because without at least one of the above, I know
my life will be a very sad thing

My Health Visitor connected me to my first counsellor. She had learnt from me that I had gone from being separated to a single mum of two sons under two years old in about 3.5 years, which caused her great concern. She could also see how little support I had as a new mum. So, she wrote me a recommendation letter to go and see a counsellor. I initially thought I wanted this for confidentiality, and because I was the only adult in my house, I wanted some mature conversation. Many people see therapy as a waste of time, but it helped me in many ways. Very early on, I learnt that many of us who are unhappy wear a mask, which I did very well. I wore mine the most when I was a child, and upon reflection, it seems that I put it on as soon as I was surrounded by people, whether I knew them or not. By the time I was in my teenage years, I was an expert at it.

I unveiled things I had not seen before my counselling sessions. I always wore this big bright and happy smile that I now understand was to ensure that all people were happy and comfortable around me. But a counsellor stopped me in one of our sessions and showed me that this was not cool. She revealed that I had told her something very hurtful that someone had said to me that crushed one of my life's biggest goals. And I was not just smiling but also laughing about this person's actions, although it was not funny. Also, I was bragging about how my grandmother taught me that my family was the be-all and end-all. Yet I was not very happy around them at that time of my life or a long time before visiting with her.

I learnt and was able to step outside of situations to reflect on the real issues. I remember being in one of my first lessons at Spelman College and being told by a professor that we, as students, should be prepared to lose relationships with friends and family. After she had finished her statement, I recall thinking to myself, oh no, not me; my friends and family love me too much to break any relationship I had with them. Unfortunately, I was wrong. Before returning to the UK, I would lose many relationships with those who were near and dear to me.

Counselling showed me that the things I was beating up on myself about were other people's problems, not mine. This would manifest itself in how I would turn up at many sessions feeling so heavy about how I had been treated. The incidents were so extreme they felt surreal. Even though I would speak about and see the benefits of letting go of their problems and stop taking their treatment of me so personally, regrettably, there was a pull that always sent me back into that toxic environment. I felt obliged to wrap up with them regardless of how it made me feel.

I spent a great chunk of my life believing that if I stayed mad at the people who hurt me, they would be hurt too. I found out that the purpose of forgiveness was for me, not them. This created such a massive shift in my life, and the author responsible for my deeper understanding and the action I took was Iyanla Vanzant. She broke this down and helped me change my world. *Forgiveness is no easy feat, but it is worth the journey.* Moreover, I read her book *One Day My Soul Just Opened Up: 40 Days and 40 Nights Toward Spiritual Strength and Personal Growth.* I remember borrowing the book from the library and reading that my life was going to change and smiled at the statement and thought that copy would be okay. Little did I know how that book would put me on a different level from where I was at the time. On the way home, I started reading the instructions on how I should read and complete the book. This advice led me to purchase my own copy. I finished that book from cover to cover. I simply could not get enough of her writings and went on to buy other books of hers. But when I think of the different disciplines in the book, forgiveness was probably one that I addressed with lip service rather than deep root cleansing as I had not fully grasped what forgiveness was going to do for my life at that time.

FORGIVING WAS AND IS HARD, BUT IT IS AWESOME

This process of forgiveness, and of course, life, are the best teachers. Plus, people have also taught me some great lessons. One of those was that I needed to consider why people may have been so mean and vicious to me. Then it would make it easier for me to forgive the reason and not stay too focused on the person. Upon reflection, I could see that I had spent so many years just going over the hurt and extreme pain that had been placed on me, and I had an ah-ha moment that showed me that what you put out, you get back. Subsequently, I was VOICING all my hurts and pains, and guess what? I was receiving new hurts and pains in my world. I also learnt that the repetition got the hurt out of my system and made me stronger. I knew this because when I retold those painful stories originally, they used to make me cry. Then the next stage was that the tears would get stuck in my throat, and the final stage would be while sharing, my eyes started watering. To me, being able to voice my life stories showed vulnerabilities in my life and empowered those with whom I shared.

MY CHILDREN

Because I received very little positive attention from those I loved dearly when I was younger, I had it in my head that I would do things very differently for my children. I did not like how the world was evolving back then, let alone today, and told myself that I did not want to have children because I did not see it fair to bring children into this world. I was accepting "love" in whatever form it came. And as the saying goes, I played with fire and got burned on three blessed occasions. One thing I knew from the first time I became pregnant was that I was too sensitive to abort a child, so my mind was made up to have all my children. As far as I am concerned, they are all blessings in my world, and

I love them sincerely. My initial counselling sessions taught me that I need not be embarrassed about having two children out of wedlock, two years apart, and being on my own. Trust me, I felt like a disappointment to everyone. Still, I realised that what I was thinking was not at all clever, especially seeing that all the women around me were practically in the same position. Why was I beating up on myself? When most of those I looked up to or held high had all done the same thing, the only difference was that I started my family later than they did—and so what?

FAMILY

One of the major issues in my life was that I left the UK to study abroad and thought the friends and family I had grown to love supported this. I felt like I was dying inside at the thought of never connecting with them on the level we were on before I left. Why were my friends and family treating me so coldly? I would ask myself. I realised that I would never really know because I did not feel the risk of rejection was worth approaching them for the answers to my questions. But there was also the case of experiencing them fobbing me off, trying to push me away, outright lying, or sweeping things under the carpet to keep secrets. If anyone tells you that there is no dysfunction in their family, they either have not seen it or are doing one or more of the above-listed things.

My counselling sessions showed me that things were not gelling too well upon my return from the USA because I stepped outside the (family and friends) circle on my own and learnt how to speak up for myself. So, I guess they were not okay with that. I must emphasise that this was a guess, as there had been little or no dialogue around this subject with my family. Since I have found my voice and started speaking up for myself, I have had very little or no contact. I need to warn you that this can happen, which can cause a lonely place in your world or your heart. Or on the other side, I have learnt to love them from afar so that I can be happy in my world and my heart. Among them was the place where I learnt to make people happy, most of, if not all my life. I had been forever jumping as high as I was told. I remember being bullied by a ginger-headed boy at school when I was little. He was always calling me a black something, which was very hurtful. I came home one day and told my significant person in my world at the time about what was happening. I was shrieked at in such a way that I knew from that very moment I would do whatever it took to make sure I never received a response like that again. This resulted in me accepting whatever issues people dumped on me or directed my way, in order to avoid rejection. Resulting in me holding in my pain because I did not believe myself to be worthy of speaking up for myself.

Many things changed positively due to my therapy and one that I was very happy with was that now if I am not happy, I let people know about it. Although it felt great each time, I must admit, initially, it was extremely scary. It would take days for me to pluck up the courage to say what I felt, but the good thing is that it got said. I always felt they would hurt me by rejecting what I had to say, so I was very uncomfortable about being vulnerable. I had grown so used to being overly concerned about a fellow man's feelings over mine that I observed myself letting so much go over the years. How I voice it today is that I would openly receive a kick in my teeth from whoever, they would ask me if I were okay, knowing full well that they had hurt me, all while I was dying inside.

Anyway, while I embraced the new me, it came at a loss of family members, as I guess they were not having the reinvented me. They were so used to telling me to jump and me responding how high that this change was not something they would take lightly. It was heart-wrenching to know that people I had placed on pedestals could run cold because I decided to better myself. I stepped out of the norm—family box—and decided to follow my dream of living abroad and gaining some degrees in subjects I loved. While abroad, I decided to author an email of closure to my mother about all the actions towards me that I deemed hateful and hurtful. She did not appreciate this and made it very clear by marrying the man I had known her to be with for most of my life and intentionally not inviting me. This was when I learnt that bullies and mean people continue such behaviours because we allow them to and keep our mouths shut. So, on finding out about the wedding, I rang friends and family worldwide to ask if I was the only person who did not know about this wedding. Some people did not respond by staying silent while I cried, and some were even told that it was my choice not to attend. I honestly thought that someone had put a dagger through my heart. To add insult to injury, I found out that my brother, who I had grown up with, tried to include my sons at his wedding party and not invite me. Wow, this was a kicker, and from this, I learnt that blood is not thicker than water. Just because you share the same blood with someone and would give your life for someone does not mean they feel the same. My sister stepped up and mediated a conversation, and we my 3 children and I managed to attend the wedding. I remember sitting at the wedding reception and names being called off the program, which did not include mine, and the MC opened the floor for people who wanted to speak. I felt so humiliated at this fact but have learnt that this was not personal to me but to whoever planned it that way.

I found that whenever out at family events, my mum would walk up to me and push her face at my mouth for me to kiss her. I always did it like a loyal lap dog, and I decided I wanted to stop this fake show because I had grown. I called my mother to ask her to stop this act as I found it uncomfortable, and as she did not answer her phone, I left a voice message. I was amazed to receive a phone call from my brother shortly after I left that message. He threatened that he would never talk to me again if I did not sort things out with my mum. He was too angry to tell me what he was told and made it very clear that he did not want to know my side of the story, so he slammed the phone down after saying what he had to say. I guess I was cut off. As I have already shared, I was going to be heard whether the person wanted to hear me or not, so I called and left a voice message giving him a piece of my mind.

I believe that everything happens for a reason, and this was such a good reason to let my mother know that her ill-treatment of me had to stop. I remember sharing with a girlfriend about the unsavoury treatment I had been receiving from my mother practically all my life. I recall her saying until I met my mum eye to eye and let her know that this would not continue. She was going to carry on treating me in this fashion. I shared the consistent pain I was getting until one day, my friend asked me, "So what are you going to do about it?" I started with the excuse of finding childcare for my baby girl. My friend offered to keep her, so my next excuse was not being sure when I could go. She responded that if I did not find this important enough to put a stop to this problem, then I should stop complaining about it because nothing would change without my actions. Therefore, I called my mum to find out if she would be in and called my girlfriend to arrange childcare for my daughter. I believe the nerves were there from the time I made the phone call to her, but it felt like the closer I got to her house, the deeper my breathing became and the the louder my heart pounded. I remember getting to her front door and still stepping on eggshells, even though my heart was in my mouth by now.

I could tell by her reception that she believed I had come to apologise for asking her not to force me to kiss her in public. Little did I know what would come from the next 20 minutes of my life because all I remember before knocking on her front door was my prayer that said, "God, please give me the right words." I let her know that my three children, who were the most important people in my world, were being impacted by her negative lifetime treatment of me and that it would stop on the day I was there at her home. This day, which I see as my new birthday, was the 4th of November 2010, and it was the day that things changed immensely for me. I informed her that her emotional, psychological, and mental abuse would also stop on that day, as that day is when I would be taking back my power. I stayed calm throughout, and I guess that was the power I was receiving from the Almighty. I heard she had told a few people that I told her that she could not speak to my children, and I felt no need to defend that because anyone who knew me, knew that that was not the truth. When I left her house that day, I had on a black coat that was pretty close to the floor in length, and although it was a cold evening, that coat was open and swinging like a cape. I felt like someone with superpowers and was now stepping on clouds, my palms dry, and my breathing and heartbeat back to their normal pace. I felt great, and had I realised how much this conversation would have changed my life, I would have had it many years prior. The real point is, all that I was holding on to was now revealed to her, and I felt great about it.

Moving on after my return from the USA was full of its adversities, but as usual, all were overcome as I knew they would have been. I came home to an empty house, one which I had left fully furnished. Someone had left the shower dripping, which leaked into the front room, causing the ceiling to fall. This was just the start, plus I had this four-month-old baby girl with me, and I had to get my sons enrolled in schools. Ultimately, I did what I felt I had to do regardless of how alone I felt, and I moved on to supporting my Baby Girl until she was safely and comfortably in the first year of infant school. I knew that supporting and being there for children during their first five years was very important, so I took full advantage of the support available. I ensured we were as sociable as possible by taking her to sing-a-longs at our local libraries and attending mother and baby groups. I also used the nursery voucher support I received from the government, which enabled us to meet more children and parents. Additionally, I always made sure I went out somewhere with our new friends during the school holidays. For myself, I completed a Leadership and Management course, parenting courses, and a GCSE in math, which incidentally, my High School math teacher had convinced me that I could not achieve.

What I feel about counsellors is that although some people feel it was a little unnecessary or excessive, I have taken counselling every year since my second child was born. It helped me through some very challenging times, so I highly recommend it to anyone considering acquiring these services. As I write this book, I am in my 27th year of being counselled, and I am not embarrassed about it either. Because it has helped me grow to become the powerful, tenacious, loving, confident, resourceful, resilient and awesome woman I am today. Through my time with many counsellors, I discovered that I was not heard when I spoke, but I was when I sang. This is probably why I was singing from such a young age. Singing, although it used to be very nerve-racking as a solo artist, is an act that has been present throughout my life. Whenever I performed, I got feedback from people stating that my voice was beautiful, which I did not initially believe. Over time, I recognised that so many people could not be hearing the same beauty if it were not true. I have now accepted that it is what it is, and I have this gift that should not be kept to myself but shared with all. I also learnt that your voice is not just to sing but also to speak, so the idea is that I will be meeting you shortly so I can elaborate on anything I have shared in this book.

9

EMPOWERMENT/CONFIDENCE/THE NEW YOU

Understanding that I spoke through singing through ninety percent of my life
Adding therapy and or counselling to my bow to help me strive

MOMENTS OF EMPOWERMENT

As an adult who is aware, I realised that the beauty in my voice is a gift from God that I must share. And how I relate this to my life is that it is also a way of saying this is what I do, who I am, and so you will hear me. Apart from the new way I conduct my life and the new friends and family I have attained along the way, the following is proof.

I started by performing at any family event because this was the space where I was always called upon to sing. These events would include birthday parties mainly and any space where we got together on special occasions such as Christmas, Easter, and christenings. Additionally, I was a member of a small group called The Faith Group, which was established in the church by my cousin. It was he, an incredibly special female friend of the family, and me. This group gave us big audiences, which was overly exciting and fulfilling for me especially being a young 8-year-old.

Another empowering phase of my life was when I joined a girl band between the age of 17 and 18. See the photo in the Jamaica Gleaner 1984. Although I cannot remember who introduced me to Lorna Fletcher's (the soloist) mum, I became a member of a girl band called The Librians and was excited about this opportunity. I was able to go out with people other than my family. I was trusted to be out there for rehearsals and actual gigs, plus I was doing something for myself rather than anyone else. Like life itself, music bands had their problems. We had to deal with the lack of punctuality and thus had to wait hours for the band members to turn up. There were always excuses as to why the band members could not be at rehearsal on time, if at all. Plus, there were many nervous experiences encountered during every performance. It was such an exciting time. It felt like I had found a new family, and because we were close in age, we could share more experiences than singing. I do not recall how many years this went on, but I remember this was an awesome time, and I felt great about myself. I went on to enroll myself in a couple of vocal workshops to gain different perspectives on what I was doing as a vocal artist. Upon reflection, I am now aware of my empowerment at the time and recognise the growth that was happening concurrently.

Knowing that I wanted to vocalise and work on what I saw as my passion, I decided to find myself a tutor. I had a great time in my vocal lessons, although I now see that I was doing much of what I was told to do, which made my voice coach happy. Keeping in mind that this was something that I did well, I was not aware if I was progressing or not. Due to my focus on whether I did the right thing or not, she was happy with the sound I was producing. My wake-up call came when I decided to apply to go on the Sky Star Search talent show. Upon the T.V. cameras' appearance, my nerves got the better of me. If I think about what was going on, I can only think that the camera, especially a TV camera, made me extra anxious. I recall being nervous and shaking so badly that the mic was hitting my teeth. What made it worse was that my outfit and makeup were great, and I flat-out bummed my performance. The judges suggested that I go and just sing at pubs, clubs, and events to get used to being in front different types of audiences. I went about my life after that and told everyone about my nightmare experience and the judges' suggestions. A vocal school called Aria School of Voice was brought to my attention and recommended by a friend.

I found someone to invite me into the fold, signed up, and found myself some more new family, which was awesome. As far as being vocally competent, this school taught me much of what I know. When I started back in the late

1980s, the school was run by an ex-member of The Chi-Lites called Eugene Thompson. I was instructed to leave Aria instead of getting kicked out because I was hiding behind the choir. We kept doing gigs, where I still wanted to stay in the choir and not sing solos. So, Eugene trained me to sing solo parts and then instructed me to leave and go do what I had been learning for the last three to four years. So, I left, went out, and performed a few private gigs on my own to get a feel of this area of the industry. However, I did not keep this up for long.

I became pregnant around the same time as I was leaving Aria. Knowing how important singing was to me, I made a conscious decision to perform as much as possible while my children were in my womb. I felt that they would at least be able to sing in tune. I remember studying Kodály during one of my summers following their births and learning that children learn just as well inside the womb as they did outside. This confirmed my thinking around me singing with my sons still inside me. I remember doing my first gig with my oldest son—still a bump in my tummy—and the song I performed was For the Love of You by Whitney Houston. My child's father and a few of my family members were there. I sang wherever and whenever there was an opportunity, whether paid or unpaid. I was not courageous enough to ask for a payment, so if they paid me, that was a bonus. The awesome part of this whole thing was listening to my sons sing back songs that were playing on the radio while still less than a year old and were totally in tune.

I joined Croydon's Black History Month Committee and started performing for them, which was something I did not expect to be part of, as the idea started as such a small thought. I learnt about this establishment while volunteering to teach a mature group of students. I was told that there were volunteer positions available on the committee. I showed my interest and was happily included. Now that I had become a part of a group that listened to some of the things I had to say and was keen to even try some of those suggestions, I felt ready to start up my own voice coaching business where I would be teaching at schools, churches, children's homes, colleges, and community centres. Once I decided that I was going to teach, I went on a mission. Not only to set up my own business because I wanted to work around my children's school hours but also so that I would not limit the many areas I could handle. I achieved this by literally ringing up my local schools and speaking to headteachers and heads of music departments. I told them what I did, and as soon as they said to come in and see us, I knew I had these jobs. I loved being able to drop my sons off at school and pick them up, plus run my business in a way that was beneficial to the three of us.

Five years before it came to fruition, I decided that I was going to live abroad. Although writing goals was not something I had learnt to do effectively, I decided on New Year's Day of 1999 to write out a list of things I wanted to achieve that year. I felt so focused on doing the right thing for my sons that I did not think much about my dreams and goals. So, I would say when they were about four and six years old, I started on this yearly list. Once the list was written, I followed up by giving each thing on that list its own page. I would list what I needed to do to attain each goal on those pages. At the start of each year, I found that I was frantically applying myself to those lists. This energy would phase out after a few weeks, even months. But the amazing thing is that when I came near the end of each year, most of the goals on my list had been achieved.

LISTEN TO THE VOICE WITHIN/ON THE RIGHT PATH

Listening to the voice within was a major challenge when no one taught me how. This was due to having every move mapped out for me except when I was at school, in athletics training, or playing a sport for my school. Not only were most things planned for me, but I never had a say in anything. Listen up, parents, we want to help our children, but we are not doing this when we do everything for them. Though I have let the guilt go, I sometimes believe I did too much for my children to a fault, especially when I felt they needed my help. I always wanted to swoop down and save them until one day, one of them said, "Mum, I do not need you to come down to the school or anything. I just want you to listen." This was so hard because all I could remember was that I did not feel protected, making me think this would not be the case for my children. But I was so busy trying not to repeat my younger experience that I ended up doing much of the same thing. Looking back, I will credit myself with the fact that my children did and still know that they are loved. I have said much of this to show that if you want something bad enough, focus on what you DO want and not on what you DON'T. The universe will give you whatever it is that you focus on.

I listened to the positive voice within that told me that it was the right time and that Spelman was the right college where I would follow my dream.

Following the three signs from my past student's uncle, the father who also made the suggestion, plus the message from the website, confirmed that I had been listening to the voice within. It is interesting that although I spent all my life involved in music, I still required signs to show me that this college was the one I would attend. It was almost as if, as soon as the message was read from the FastWeb website, I knew that this was where I was going, and from there, I was on a mission.

There were also loud signs that showed me this was my path. I remember picking up my sons, who were 9 and 11 years old at the time, and moving to Atlanta, Georgia, to pursue a BA in Music Performance. Despite all the adversities I experienced, I just kept pushing. Through the eviction and having to consider a woman's shelter; the lack of money at the time; the hard time my youngest son was having in schools, where I had to move him three times plus home-school for a year; picking up the oldest from police custody at 3 am, although I still had a relatively small voice. I knew a bigger voice was required, plus great courage, to let the Police know they were wrong. I was also worried about why a previous employer told me to wait while she sorted things out for me to start work for her. Only to find out that she knew full well she had no intention of employing me that year. God spoke to me about getting paid to work in music, for the Jazz Ensemble, to be exact, which was awesome. Plus, there were many more challenges faced living in a foreign country for five years.

There are some adversities that could have caused me to return home without a degree or broken my path thus far. For example, take the situation around the Chair of the Music Department giving me an ultimatum about changing my academic path. This conversation took place during my 5th year of college. It was the voice within that led me to the decision to change my degree. Then, with God's grace, I graduated at the same time as my music degree peers. This showed me that I was supposed to do a Comparative Women's Studies Major degree and was also blessed with a minor in Music Performance. I graduated with a 3.4 GPA even though I completed it while I was about seven and a half months pregnant.

Money was one of my greatest challenges, and as usual, God stepped up every semester, even though I was always told by many members of staff that I needed to go home. Thanks to Mrs. Rosa McQuay of Spelman College, I was shown many places to apply for funding, and wherever she could assist, she helped me with applications. I gained money from John Lennon, Avon, Pauline

Drake (PEDS), Dean Scholarships, and more. Additionally, I found work on campus at Spelman's Fitness Centre and Spelman's Jazz Ensemble. I was told that the school could not help me financially, literally every semester. However, I still managed to complete a degree that cost £100k, to which I contributed very little financially. So, I will happily thank Spelman College for the exponential growth I experienced there, as it also helped shape the woman I am today.

Even though I practiced teaching from home before establishing my business, I remember deciding early on that I would continue to gain an education to serve my students better. I did this by rising to the occasion wherever the opportunity presented itself. Additionally, it would enhance my students' learning and improve and grow not just my vocal ability but my musical ability. To achieve this, I pursued and completed the following teacher courses because I wanted to feel more comfortable within the teaching environment, both musically and academically. So, as well as the occasional weekend music workshops and Kodály, I also gained a Certificate in Education to create a curriculum and learn how to assess my students to notate their growth. I also completed a Facilitators Access to music course, which allowed me to work with a private school and bring the students in my course together to produce a show. It was awesome, and for me, community spirit is what gets positive results, and I did not have to think about what-ifs, buts, or maybes. I just needed to take one step after another.

I found that many of my female students were trying to perform with baggage preventing their best performances, which led me to take a Counselling Course. I took the first three levels to learn what questions to ask and how to approach my clients to lessen their load and sing or speak at their best. It was extremely empowering to help pupils see how they could permit themselves to take back their power from those less worthy. From running my voice business here in the UK, I went on to achieve a BA in Women studies—a concentration in music, and a Minor in music performance, which was not the plan. Though this was another thing I learnt from goal setting and going for your dreams, they never went according to how you planned them. Once I had discovered this, I realised that not attaining the full goal was not a failure. I returned to the UK as a single mother of three children, having accomplished two degrees from a country where initially I only knew the family who had accommodated me for the first few days after my arrival. I think I did darn well, to be honest.

I have always asked questions about any information I was given that sounded interesting to me. So, while doing my weekly or bi-weekly visits to the Income Support Department, my advisor heard my concerns about the difficulties I found in bettering myself with such a young child. She introduced me to a college that specifically taught female single parents and provided childcare. Therefore, I asked the questions, made the connection, and spoke to the appropriate people who managed to enroll me in a Leadership Course that I attended on the weekends. I would travel to my classes on Friday afternoon, which would last throughout the weekend. The college accommodated us (the students), fed us and made childcare provisions while we were studying, plus they funded it, which was awesome. I enjoyed this course so much that I want to establish and take this concept to another level in the future when I establish myself financially. The next course I found myself in was a Parenting Course because I felt I was flailing and needed help in this predicament. It was and is challenging being a parent when there are two of you, yet alone one. So here I was, looking for support, and yes, I received this and enjoyed it immensely. I was doing my favourite thing: learning and not worrying about payment for my studies or childcare; what more could I have asked for?

Although my MA in Education was not where my education stopped, it was the official time-based, on-campus type of education I willingly experienced. What I love about this experience was that I had grown so much that I felt ready to embark on this new venture with my five-year-old daughter in tow. The adversity came before I left the country, in that they needed proof of a certain amount of money before sending the paperwork needed to acquire my I20 document. I wrote the Texas Woman's University an email explaining how they would receive their money from me, with literally nothing completely confirmed. But it all worked out as I had stated. Plus, there was $1000 more than I had accounted for, so God was with me all the way. I met with many adverse situations that took a toll on me, but by the grace of God, I managed to come out to the other end. I passed on what I had learnt, to one-to-one students and groups and saw them grow from it. Not only was this immensely rewarding, but it had raised my confidence vastly.

10

WHERE LIFE HAS TAKEN ME NOW

*To a point where empowerment, confidence, and
The New You and I are blooming
Where Life has taken me now can be described as
nothing less than booming*

For me, it was crazy that the US made such a big deal about not accepting bullying in their school system because my daughter was having such a challenging time with students, teachers, and even a principal. The last straw was when she screamed so hard for me not to leave her at school. I did not need to see more of that display of hurt and terror on her face. I remember telling her that she did not need to be manhandled and that she should go to her class and calm down. However, the screaming continued. I remember looking at the principal and saying, "Just give me my child." She asked me if I was sure. I was so sure that no child behaves like this just to get out of going to school, so things must have been bad. I worked to get our flight money together, and we returned home, as I knew this school environment could not be healthy for her.

As I was subbing while in the US, I thought I would focus on this area when I returned to the UK. The intention was to hit the road running upon my return, and I started contacting teaching agencies in the UK to see what paperwork I needed to bring with me to start. Unfortunately, I was misinformed and told I could not do anything until I got back, and I would not need anything to prove myself here, as I was a UK national. This misinformation cost me time and money, which was very disconcerting. I did need paperwork from the US government, and I made the application to them, but I needed to wait until this all came through to get work. Eventually, I subbed but not around music, which is what I do best. Although subbing in academics was not my specialty, I went ahead with it as it was something I was doing in the USA anyway. Plus, I wanted to be able to earn an income as I was informed that I could not get any help from the system, having been out of the country for a set time.

Unfortunately, my daughter ended up in a school where she was bullied again. We spoke about being positive, and I was assured by the new school that it would be different this time. Although the Head emphasised that this would never happen at her school. This vicious little girl had been bullying her class since year two, so I guess my daughter's bright and vibrant spirit was one she despised. This showed me the lip service that schools were so good at when it came to bullying. Because most parents had their kids threatened by this girl until year 6, the same behaviours were still being accepted. I approached the Head and her class teacher, and still no joy. So, two weeks into her second term, I pulled her out and homeschooled her. It turned out that all the ailments keeping my daughter out of school were her psychological creation to protect herself from this child. We would visit the doctors almost weekly and the A&E Department every month, even twice in some cases. We did every test we could think of, or so the doctor said, and they all came back negative. Eventually, I signed her up with a counsellor myself as the system's counselling service informed us that my daughter was not the type of child they would deal with. I know that I saw a different child once I pulled her out of the school. All the problems of having her at home without gaining new employment dissipated after I saw the difference. She became calm, less anxious, and much more talkative and enjoyable to be around. The action that also made me melt was when her counsellor said that on their first session in January, even though she had already been seeing my daughter for three months, it was the first time she heard her laugh. Her counsellor acknowledged and respected me for making such a bold move and reassured me that this was the best move I could have made for Kimani. I truly believe that it was.

While working at getting back into the swing of things here in the UK, I decided to establish another business here so I could work around my daughter and serve the people I wanted to work for in a way I knew best. I realised that even though you may start things with the greatest intentions, this does not mean it was purpose-made for you. During the summer, I volunteered in the areas I loved, specifically with children. People were happy for me to continue to volunteer, but I found that they took advantage of my generosity for longer than I had intended. Subsequently, I put a deadline on when I would stop volunteering and start charging. Unfortunately, they decided not to use my service, and I ended up with no clients. I managed to do everything I needed to run the business, but as I write this, I still have no clients. This was starting to take its toll on my psyche because I had been back in the UK for nearly two years and still had no work. It had gone past frustration, especially as I put so many hours into things that were not working out.

DETACHMENT

I have been forced to detach myself from what I believe to be negative people, toxic environments, and people who just do not love or care for me. I was working at being whatever my sons wanted me to be because I felt that this was how mothers were supposed to behave. When I became aware that many positive and loving gestures were being replaced with negative disrespectful ones, it was time to detach. I chose to believe that detaching from people did not mean cutting them off, never speaking to them again, but more like loving them from afar. I had made up my mind that I no longer wanted to be anyone's punching bag, and to get that, I had to go through feeling bad about this move but doing it anyway. I blocked phone calls from my sons as they both knew where I lived, and things became less stressed and more peaceful in my world. When it came to family, I was brought up by my grandmother and was taught that they were the be-all and end-all of life itself. What I learnt about my specific family is that I should stay in the lane they knew to be mine, but once I stepped out of that lane, I would be on my own. Hence, I took that risk and found another lane as I pursued major and different goals that interested me, not them. I paid the price of hurt, loneliness, pain, and much more, and I will put my hand on my heart today and tell anyone it was worth it.

As far as friends go, when I was coming up in school, my so-called friends would get so upset when they heard me telling people that I did not have any friends and that I only had associates. This was because my friends were forever hurting me, and as this was not how I would treat a friend, I was not going to accept that treatment. As I reflected on friendships, I noted that those I have held nearest and dearest are the ones who hurt me the most. Some have taken such advantage of the sincere person that I was and still am that they did not even think I should have a problem with their mistreatment of me. When I first heard Erykah Badu's line in her song, *Appletree,* where she says, "I pick my friends like I pick my fruit." I never quite understood that. Now I know that everyone has their interpretation of what they have heard; I understand it to mean that. For example, I would pick up bananas and look for bruises and scratches, and if these were visible, I would return them and pick one up that was free of these. The bruises and scratches are what I would refer to as negatives and disrespectfulness from a friend or family member.

I no longer give people power over me or chase after them to make them happy. This is a statement I often think about and make a point to follow. Since returning to the UK, I have been more focused on cleaning out toxic people who dull my environment. Although it has been extremely hard, it has made life easier. When those near and dear to you have not noticed that you have left the country for nearly two years, that is when you do not need any more confirmation from them that, in their eyes, you are not worthy. Plus, if you are in a foreign place where you do not have to see them anyway, this made it easier to go back home to the UK and not be impacted by not seeing them even after having been back here for nearly two years.

LOVING YOURSELF

I have been working on loving myself more than usual and have displayed this action in more than one way. I have woken up to the fact that I was more worthy than people gave me credit. Here are some examples of how I have grown to love myself:

- Realising that no matter the label, or role that people have or play in your life, it does not give them the right to mistreat, disrespect, hurt, or bully you.
- Upon Reflection, I started clarifying to people that I would no longer accept their awful and shameful behaviours and ill-treatment towards

me. In many cases, this was very painful, lonely, hurtful, and isolating, especially when I would be reminded of some good times through someone's words or actions or something I was watching.

+ I do my best to take myself out monthly (usually to the cinema).

+ I meditate first thing every morning for 18 minutes, followed by a daily prayer or three.

+ Then I list things I am grateful for in my online gratitude journal, which is rarely or never material things. Because I believe that if I have the spiritual area in place and command more of that by being grateful for that, then the materials will follow.

+ I have cleared many, or should I say 99% of people from my world that were not treating me like the Queen that I was and still am. Because we must not forget we need some of those unsavoury characters around to help us grow.

MY EMPRESS, MY MIRACLE BABY

+ I got over the fact that I was in my early 40s and gracefully accepted the blessing in the form of an Empress.

+ Absorbing and loving the fact that my baby girl was and still is:
  - ❖ Loving
  - ❖ Tenacious
  - ❖ Determined
  - ❖ Super smart
  - ❖ Beautiful
  - ❖ Humble
  - ❖ A GREAT singer
  - ❖ Wanting to hang out with me
  - ❖ Teachable
  - ❖ Affectionate
  - ❖ Independent
  - ❖ A brilliant communicator—I always find myself saying from the mouth of babes and conversationalist—even in these times.
  - ❖ Fun and comedic

✦ Although I panicked and visited three different doctors' offices to confirm my pregnancy, I fully accepted that this was a fact once I got the same date from all three. I saw this as a way of loving myself because it lessened the stress and put me in a place where I could prepare for my little miracle. Plus, even though I did not know what to expect at this age, as it was 14 years since I had last been pregnant, I have been sent an amazing amount of joy, hope, and understanding to my world. My Baby Girl is wise beyond her years and always gives me a little more to think about, and even when she challenges me, I walk away and think about how much I need to back off so that she can find her voice as I did. I dreamt and hoped that she would not take as long as her mummy did because of how much I love, adore, and feel her in the depth of my heart. I feel I am going to be, and I am currently so proud of this young lady.

ACTIONS SPEAK LOUDER THAN WORDS

Although the phrase says, "Actions speak louder than words," I will still go as far as to say that if you are not being vocal, you may as well be invisible. If people do not see you, then how can they hear you? I was so quiet when I wanted something for myself or needed someone's actions to change that people would speak on my behalf and do whatever they wanted to do in my life.

I thought I was invisible as a toddler, but those "hairbrush" performances got me through those years of hiding. I was actually heard while I performed all those years ago, but unfortunately, it was someone else's words because I was always singing the songs of other artists. Although I could and can write poems that lead to songs, I would and always performed other artists' songs. This was the lack of confidence to be vulnerable and put my life into words. I sang other songs just as I lived my life for others until I stepped up and said no to those abusing my love and kindness.

Additionally, although I produced very nervous performances in the past, I have found that all the vocal performances have shaped my life healthily and positively. Therefore, the presentations are nowhere near as nervous as they used to be. I have found that a small amount of nerves are always good as it keeps the adrenalin pumping to give your presentation that little bit more pizazz.

DO NOT FEAR RECORD COMPANIES

When I was younger, I remember being told by a wise and experienced singer that she had a number two record in the charts for six weeks and never made a penny. I was also taught at vocal school that major record companies would sign you up; however, if they had another artist they were trying to sponsor who was similar to you, they would put your record on the shelf and promote the other artist. After hearing both stories, I decided that no record company would screw me like this and ended up doing nothing. What I now understand from those stories is that they were not shared with me to prevent me from doing anything but to be forewarned. I have also learnt that one woman's experience may be similar but will never be the same as mine. So, always take risks that are not life-threatening because we learn from our so-called mistakes. I believe we all travel a personal road in life and will always come to forks on that road. Do not spend too long at that fork because even if you take the wrong path, life will always lead you back to the correct one. One thing, though, is that you must lessen the amount you take on or are doing in your life, because you must be awake to hear which path you are supposed to take. With too many things going on, you will miss the lessons needed to move forward and down the right path. Therefore, some people take longer than others to grow up and get to that comfortable place where they live their life's purpose.

EMPOWERING OUR VOICES

This is not just about showing you how to use your voice as a vocalist or a speaker to the best of your ability but how the voice can support you throughout your life, such as:

-   Teach you things about yourself. I have spent over 90% of my life teaching, performing, and studying voices. And music has shown me where I have come from as this tiny mouse to where I have travelled over the years and currently stand as this powerhouse. Get out of your head and do not rely on people to give you your power and stipulate what constitutes power. You are great, you are loved, and you are awesome.

- You are also human, so stop letting people guilt you into doing or being what you no longer want to do or be. Or guilt you out of being treated with the worthiness you so deserve. Stop thinking about your mistakes and how those shameful things could become public if you change. Like anything else, it is better out than in. You will probably find that once the naysayers get hold of and reveal your secrets, give it a few days or weeks, and it will soon become old news, and then they are onto the next person's drama.

- It can save you from worst-case scenarios. When I first arrived at Spelman College, while my first year was ending, not having been away from my family for this long, I decided that I wanted to go back and visit during the summer. As usual, money was the defining factor. What I know now that I did not realise back then was that you must be careful about what you speak out to the universe. Also, when you understand how that works, it puts you in such a powerful place. I spoke to some friends about wanting to go home and not having enough money to do so, and the suggestion was put out there to contact someone they thought could help. The woman ran the Children's Dance and Drama summer school at Spelman College. I approached her, and she was keen for me to come and tutor the kids for a period. She told me to think about what I wanted to teach them and how much I would charge. Another lesson I gained is worthiness.

- I asked friends and tutors at the college what they thought would be a good price to charge. I remember someone stating that I could not charge more than $15 per hour. Although I was asking, I was still thinking that I left the UK charging £35 for one-on-one students, so I did not think that charging such a low amount for a group of about sixteen students would be reasonable. So, I approached her with the highest amount I could semi-comfortably say out of my mouth, and when she accepted my quote, I nearly choked. While we continued to converse, she later asked me to remind her of the amount as to whether it was $50 more than I had asked her for. I taught for a week or two and was able to make up our fares to travel to the UK and visit as I had spoken into existence.

- Your voice can also produce some awesome opportunities—I remember approaching the headmaster of a Church of England School where

I correctly assumed they would only have a classical choir. It did not take long to realise that the Head of Music would not support me. So, I prayed for everything to go as well as I could manage, and in return, I had all the parents of the 45-piece choir on my side. I established a gospel choir and managed to get them to perform at the next Black History Month gig in replacement of my usual act. Before we knew it, we were asked to perform at many of the places where the classical choir would normally have performed. Plus, other people who had attended our initial performances, also asked us to present at their events.

The above are examples of where I had to speak up, if not directly to people, then out to the universe. Using your voice as it is supposed to be used should allow you to speak, be heard, and understand how to communicate your specifics correctly the first time. It has taken me years to speak my truth, but I believe it has been due to the baggage I have been getting rid of along the way. So, parents, please be aware that allowing your children to speak when they are young does not mean they can be disrespectful. It means allowing the space for them to express themselves, which is best done when both parties are calm. There is a caution that I want to throw at you, which is that some of you may have heard the phrase, "Be careful what you ask for because you just might get it." As far as the universe goes, the way it works is that whatever you focus on or give energy to, whether internal or external, the universe WILL give it to you.

Hence, when you agree with someone on something you do not believe in, it will not happen on your part. An example is when people are in a relationship, and one says they want children, and the other agrees, but no baby is manifesting. One of the partners may not want children, but they still want to be in the relationship. I have heard of instances where partnerships have dissolved, and the partner who wanted to have children manages to have a child with a new partner with no problems. Fortunately, the universe does not work immediately. It gives you a little time to increase your energy to a point where you have made it clear that this is what you want. Also, please remember, if you focus on something you DO NOT want, the universe will give you that too. Therefore, you must be careful. For all those women swearing that they would not go out with a certain type of man, that is who you will end up with.

THE LOVE OF MY LIFE

And I mean that this man was the complete, sincere and genuine love of my whole life. I reflected upon the partners that I had in my past and concluded that this was it. So, let us go back and first see what I was thinking: to speak my desires into the universe with confidence and manifest love into my world. Okay, so I had pretty much arrived at a stage in my life where I had decided that I would live out my time being a successful single mother of three children as there was no one in my life then. I knew I was doing something that was preventing the man that God planned for me from entering my life. Many of my friends and associates asked me what I had done differently that allowed him in this time around. I could not be specific, but upon reflection, the following four points were what I spoke about and acted on with conviction.

- I touched and agreed (fist bump) with my daughter about six months before meeting him that we would get this awesome daddy/hubby to-be (never forget to add the 'to-be' at the end of your agreement if you want a husband because the universe could give you someone else's husband, which is not what you want) by Christmas. This was a habit I picked up from my younger brother in Fort Lauderdale. He said it is a Scripture from the Bible, Matthew 18:20.
- My daughter and I then went on to write a list of how he would conduct himself, look like, and what characteristics he would have. It included things like being loving, a ffectionate, caring, a provider, protector, fun, funny, one-man woman, God-fearing, non-smoker, has his own teeth, his kids were old enough to take care of themselves, no baby mama drama, and all the rest. I stressed specificity earlier because although I got much of what I wanted and more, some areas were still not covered. Fortunately, I have learnt to accept him with all his flaws, just as he has accepted mine.
- I made a space on the right-hand side of my closet for his clothes. I learnt this over time but never really believed it or took it literally. I also learnt to put that list we had created in my underwear draw. My attitude by then was, what do I have to lose?

⊥ Then the biggest, most challenging activity was, once the list was made and all the above was done, I would leave all thoughts and actions about it alone.

My daughter and I went about our business dealing with the adversities that were sent our way. There were times when I doubted and had thoughts that maybe Christmas was a little too soon. I also want to express that when I made the list, there were thoughts of how I did not have time for a man in my life anyway. This thought came because my daughter was too young to take care of herself, and I was also thinking about starting a business. So, one day I was overly excited about having found my cousin, who I love dearly. I had lost contact with him and had just seen him on Facebook. He mailed me his phone number to make contact. I was contacting him for the first time at work, and I could hear someone in the background asking about me.

My cousin let me know who it was and asked if I could remember him after giving me several scenarios where this man and I had met before when I was much younger. I was a little embarrassed because I could not recall one of the reminders he had given me. Anyway, he asked my cousin to give me his phone number, and I hesitated about making that call. I called my cousin several times and fobbed this guy off, saying I could not find his number and making other excuses. Then he asked for my number, which I tentatively allowed my cousin to give him. We moved from talking on the phone to speaking about meeting up with each other. Again, I spent a few weeks pushing him away with the excuse that I had very little time and could not find childcare. He was being very gentlemanly about my refusals but continued going with the flow. On the other hand, my cousin got mad and told him to pay for the childcare. And let me just say that his words were not said calmly. This man was more than happy to pay, just so he could go on a date with me, so I found the childcare and arranged to meet him. The same week of the meeting, he asked me for a photo of myself, and I reluctantly sent one. Then I asked for one from him and texted him back, saying he looked scary. We managed to laugh it off and went ahead with our first date.

Neither of us drove, so we took public transport as the venue was close to where I lived. I judged him by his cover and tried to avoid him when I got on the bus, but I could not avoid him after remembering that I had sent a photo that week. We met and had a great conversation, and if I am honest, I believe that I was starting to feel this man during our phone conversations. The big one for me was when I told him I was only interested in a long-term relationship. In fact, one that would see me to the end of my days, plus the fact that marriage was a requirement. After stating all that, I expected to have chased him away, but he still called me back the next day. I say all this to stress how my past was having me push him away to the point that, when we were on our date, I made this awful speech, which I regret. I told him I was not feeling him, felt no chemistry, and did not expect to see him again after that day. On the way home from the date, I remember waiting until the last few seconds before getting up for my bus stop so that I would not have to do a long-drawn-out goodbye. Unbelievably, he still called and began to irritate me by referring to me as if I were his girlfriend. I was highly uncomfortable with this. While the calls continued, I kept convincing myself that he was not for me.

This man spoke so sincerely and genuinely that I had to start checking myself until I realised that he was exactly what God sent for me. And here I was, trying to push him away. It seemed so crazy, but I know many of you are allowing your past to cloud your judgement. Moreover, I had never been out with a man that sounded like he had stepped off the boat yesterday, in that his Jamaican accent was so thick. Plus, even though I was no longer in contact with the family I grew up with, parts of me felt that they would not have approved. This was so crazy to think that a set of people I moved from, at least 15 years prior, was still impacting my actions.

Anyway, I began to check myself and open my heart to the love that was oozing my way. Every awesome action he showed me, thoughts he wanted for us, and characteristics about him in general just threw me through a loop. Because for as long as I can remember, I have always had to look out for myself and the people around me. It had never been the other way around, even more since I left home. Do not get me wrong; I am not trying to play the martyr here because I enjoy serving people very much and seeing them happy made my day. It was in my DNA to be a giver and a caretaker, and I did so very well. Therefore, to have a man show up in my world who did not even need to be asked if I wanted to be supported, provided for, loved, respected, treated like his queen and more, just sent my head spinning. I had thoughts of being drawn to him and loving him.

He showed me what the phrase, "it's the little things that count" really meant. The small gestures, like making sure I had money to take care of the little things, added up for me. When we would go to his home on the weekends, we would stop by the shop on the way in. He would buy everything he thought we needed, or I wanted so that I would not have to worry about anything if he had to go to work the following day. He directly refused to stay, visit, or sleep over at my home until we had a date with my daughter to make sure that she knew and was comfortable with him when she saw him in the mornings. So, we soon arranged for that to take place.

He was less nervous than I was, which was a bonus, and as soon as we walked away from the date, she put her thumbs up and said she liked him because he was fun and funny. I had such a hard time with my daughter during that year. She would go to bed sick and wake up too sick to go to school, which was the case for most of the year that she was present at her primary school. I remember for weeks, if not months, he would be on the phone talking with us until it was time for me to leave her bedroom. He gave all kinds of advice, tips, and concoctions that we could try. She was so in awe of him that she asked him, in what appeared to be less than three months, if she could call him daddy. I was so shocked. I tried to tell her how this was a little early and thus inappropriate, only to be told by him to be quiet, as the question was addressed to him, not me. He told her that he would be honoured for her to call him daddy. I nearly cried as all we asked for was coming true.

During early conversations in our relationship, I remember being a little judgmental about his goal of wanting to go on a cruise with his family. Then realizing that he was an absolute family man made this goal very befitting. Then I learnt there were a few things on my list that he did not tick off. I found them quite concerning, such as him not believing in God (although he did believe in a higher force), being a smoker, and his attitude or approach to life appearing abrupt and rugged to me at the time. What I learnt about my major issue with him not believing in God was that you really cannot change who people are, and he was showing me so much love that I had to believe that he was the one. I realised he was a diamond in the rough, and so now was the time when I would have to demonstrate what I wanted to see in him. Subsequently, I relaxed and opened myself to be gentle, affectionate, and loving towards him and gradually received the same treatment.

I loved that I could be myself and say what I needed to without him holding it against me. I would not receive threats to leave the relationship, which was the case in many of my past unions, when people were not pleased with me communicating my truth. Christmas was amazing because it was the most stressless, loving one I had in my entire independent life, and it felt great. The only things I remember praying aloud for were to be able to buy presents for him and my daughter—ones that they were not expecting. I recall going Christmas shopping with him and feeling a little low, as a part of me felt like he was taking away my job as her parent. How sick was that! He bought clothes for my daughter and took care of absolutely all the food. It was just that I had never had this treatment before. He always knew when something was wrong, and when I decided to share, he frequently wanted to help or solve the issue himself. He sure helped me solve my daughter's bedtime issues which impacted her health and resulted in less frequent asthma attacks. His assistance lessened my stress and gave me more sleep, leading to a calmer, higher spiritual presence.

Lockdown was a major wake-up call. It allowed me to learn about my new love and to see if this was someone I wanted to spend the rest of my life with. Plus, see if he could be the right dad for my daughter. Additionally, if I were in such a comfortable place, my stress levels about being out of work would lessen. I am a firm believer in energy levels; the lower the energy, the more likely negatives come into play. In those five months that he stayed over, I would say about three or four major issues came up where the first thing I thought was that this could break what we had. But because we were able to communicate, discuss the issues, and state what we felt we needed to do in the future to avoid reoccurrence and keep it moving to a positive place, we held things together. He is a very upbeat, hi-energy, jovial, calm, loving, and relaxed man, who I genuinely believe, within my core, that I want to spend the rest of my life with.

TRY MY COURSE

I would like you to try the course and see how it can benefit you while using your voice in communication and presentation for recital or speech purposes. Additionally, I feel confident that this will be a bonus in your life in general. There are numerous ways that this could help you. I can see you now building confidence enough so that you will grow each time you perform or present your voice on a one-to-one level or in front of an audience. I hope you can see all the benefits and growth spurts in my life and relate the steps in the course to how you could grow in your own life. Breathing is the foundation of life itself, and when slowed down, it can be used to support everything that comes out of your mouth, and you will achieve a positive result. The course will help you articulate and phrase yourself precisely so that you should be fully understood, thus giving your audience a greater, more meaningful experience.

Therefore, breaking down the song is necessary, as it prepares you for any mishaps that may happen and makes you stronger if or when life does not go to plan. Furthermore, posture plays an important part because when this is off, this takes a toll on your body and, thus, your performance. Once more, when you are tired, things in life and your presentation get tough, resulting in a challenging performance, or you sometimes end up not addressing things in your life. Remember that our body is our instrument, so look after it, and it will look after you in return. A stage is like life. You are always presenting yourself, and at voice school, I learnt that you are as good as your last performance. So, work on practicing stage presence and the rest of the course until the keys become natural to you. Then you will always be putting your best self forward.

Counselling has played a major part in my life. It was a space where I could experience adult interaction and repeat my past traumas, hurts, and pain to the same people without being judged or ridiculed. This was major because even though I may have shared some sensitive things with friends and family, at some stage, I would have these things kicked back in my face privately or publicly. Either way, I was put back to square one because I would have to wipe some more mess out of my life. Just like my performances, I realised that although I may have been repeating many of my issues vocally, I finally grew out of those repetitive habits. As I grew, my performances became more confident, and my life seemed to fall into place at the same time. I learnt that not only was my life improving as I spoke out and shared what I felt, but I was also expressing songs in a way that had greater meaning. Thus, I was killing two birds with one stone; both the counselling and the vocal performances enhanced my growth in life.

IT IS TIME TO AUTHOR THIS BOOK

I must admit that I have been considering authoring a book for many years. The film, The Secret, showed me that when you raise your energy to something, you must believe that thought during its materialisation. I also kept mentioning it to people who were mainly recommending that I find a ghost-writer. Thinking that only an author or a ghost-writer could write a book, I had made up my mind that I did not have enough time to achieve this goal. I always envisioned authors going away to a house in the country for a long while, where they were in complete solitude. Besides, I believe that everything happens for a reason, plus nothing ever happens before its time (Mama always said this). So here I am sharing my course and a bit of myself with you so that you can hopefully live to your full potential.

Three is my lucky number, and it is something that occurs in my life quite frequently. This was the same thing when it came to writing this book. Firstly, while living abroad, I went to a social media course and found out about a man from the UK who was going to be able to show us how to write a book. Although I knew that your goals did not have to include how you were going to get money to finance your venture, I let money stop me from writing my book at that time.

Secondly, I was online minding my own business when I found a course that looked perfect and, again, would help me write my book. And as I always said, this looked like the ideal way to do this. Miracles kept popping up; a young lady I had given my business card to at the initial 3-hour workshop called me. It was to share her sign-up offer, which permitted her to bring someone with her on the full intensive weekend, and she chose me. She offered to allow me to pay her a certain amount, and we could both do the course. Then something did not feel right, and on asking her to clarify some questions, I found out that I could not join her because I was at the initial seminar. Although very disappointing, it was not my time. At least, this was how I saw it.

Finally, while online, I got hooked on a five-day book challenge, and since completing the course, I started writing something in my book close to every day. I realised this was the right time because I woke up each morning thinking about writing more content. As I write this, I am still without clientele for my business, which I had established just over a year ago and is another reason I am writing this book. Sixteen years ago, just before I left to study abroad, I was charging £35 per hour and came back to the UK to find out that local voice coaches were now charging £15-£30 per hour. I could not see myself charging less than £60 and saw that people paid more attention to money than quality.

This man's five-day book challenge stood out for me because he covered absolutely everything you needed to know about writing and distributing a book. How to plan, write, fund, publish, and move it. He was very ethical and did not shortcut us in any way. He offered services to help you or even do it for you, and little or none of the 10 hours was spent on promoting himself. He showed us how writing a book was not about selling books but more about becoming an authority on our subject and giving people the confidence to want to purchase big-ticket items from us. His energy levels were amazingly high, which was just what I needed at that time in my life. Plus, he made me believe this was a possibility, and here I am, making this next part of my dream come true.

My dream was to find the next path to my purpose, and I genuinely believe I am on the right road. I will be able to use this book to speak at events and show people how possible it is to achieve your every goal by using some or all these steps. Therefore, I feel like this is what I need to be doing to show people that if you want something bad enough, you can absolutely make it happen.

ABOUT THE AUTHOR

 **Y**vonne Dacres is the owner of Empowering Our Voices, a Vocal artist, Vocal coach, a lifelong learner, and has dabbled in acting. She's best known for bringing silence to a noisy crowded room when she opens her mouth to sing. She loves to serve people, and always wants the best for them. So, seeing how working on her own and with various other voices, has empowered and impacted many things in our lives, positively. She now wishes to share her life's many experiences, including the vocal course with audiences who also want to improve themselves.

Dacres was born in and currently resides in Surrey, England with her family.

Since returning to education in 1995 she has studied, taught, and performed in the area of voices for 25 plus years, both in England and the USA. Gaining her MA in Education, her BA in Women Studies, and Minor in Music Performance in the USA.

What she has found while working with her clients, whether they be one-to-one, groups or choirs, is that they have always grown in at least one area of their lives. Coaching them how to confidently use their voices, whether singing or speaking has led them to attain big dreams into their lives.